HOW A FOREIGNER CAN

BE SUCCESSFUL IN AMERICA

Be A Millionaire

By Paul J. Toyle

FIRST EDITION

To my wife Martha Desormis, son Kevin Toyle

And my daughter Wendy P. Toyle

Contents

Preface

It would be selfish if I failed to share my success with the rest of the world. As the first person in my family to immigrate in the United State, I left a legacy for the rest to follow. Although I was not born and raised in a wealthy family, my mind has always been rich with great thoughts and dreams. I always dreamed of being a leader and being in the highest social position; the highest rank, and the highest elevation. I never stop thinking, dreaming, and acting.

I don't have a perfect past, but I have always contemplated my future with the trust I have in God and my desire for success. My childhood was not as great as I expected it to be, due to some unpleasant things that happened to my eyes and not being able to do a thing about them, but I never let it hold me back while I continued on and marched toward my destiny.

I was born in the Caribbean into a moderate family with six children. My dad was a house builder and he was the only one working in the family while my mom stayed at home to do household work and take care of the children. The two things my family valued the most were school and church. They were very religious people and instilled in their children the great value of religion, which is why I am so religious to this day. School was of great importance in society and it was considered a great activity for people to wake up at dawn and to prepare for school, make the students review their books and start the day with some breakfast that mom prepared and packed up for the journey to school.

Life was very hard and extremely difficult for uneducated people and I will say that those who did not have a chance to be educated believed that education was the key factor to success. This means, of course, that they wanted to make sure that their children would not have to go through the same illiterate life, but to be well equipped with an education to provide the tools for a better life.

Public schools were scant and the quality of education was poor, to say the least. However, most people were obligated to pay private schools for their children whether they could afford to pay or not. We saw those who could not afford to pay for basic food nutrition for their families, but who were forced to pay private schools for their children, always with the expectation that when the children grew up they could become doctors, engineers, or nurses to help mitigate the painfully poor lifestyles of their families.

During my childhood, it would be fair to say that I did not have too much fun because not only did the country not offer this kind of atmosphere for kids to enjoy, but my family was financially deprived. Some of the things we did for fun included swimming into a rocky river, or playing soccer on the dusty ground in hopes we might find a little space suitable in people's yards, at school, or in church yards. Most of the time our play did not include a real ball or even real shoes to wear. It was only our bare feet because we could not afford a real soccer ball or shoes to wear. We would never dare to wear the same shoes we wore to school or church. You see, if we got caught we would get a severe whooping from our parents with a rod, a belt, or anything that they could get their hands on. I can't forget to mention that playing dominos was another amusement our neighbors loved to do. The youth were assembled, along with older people, all sitting at the same table talking about all kinds of subjects while playing. Of course, sometimes the game was halted because of some great argument or even some emotionally-charged fist fights.

 The faith I have in God and the very hopeful spirit I have surely combined which have helped me go through all the adversity in my life and to became a survivor. When I became a police officer at the age of twenty-one and was paid the first check that I ever worked for -- it was about time! Luckily, my country's government signed a contract with the U.S government for the new recruit's as police officers to travel to the United State for training purpose. My group was the first to travel to the U.S onboard a military air plane to a military base that served as a training camp and located in Missouri. That was an exciting moment that I will never forget and was a major break through for me, knowing that my life would never be the same. That was the beginning of a changing life for me. After spending three years in the police force serving my country and my community, I decided not to renew the contract with the police institution because I knew that was not the final point of achievement in my life, so I made a request to the U.S embassy to renew my visa, which was accepted.

I traveled back to the United States for the second time, this time on my own where I started learning a new culture, with new people, a new language, new atmosphere, and the chance to live a new life. This is the place where I pursued my dream as a foreigner to become successful.

I attended Chattahoochee Technical College of Georgia where I graduated in 2008 with a Biomedical Engineering Technology Degree. I was accepted at Liberty University of Virginia where I also graduated in 2011 with a Degree in Science of Religion.

You can do it too. Just read the book entirely and you'll find useful instructions about how to become a millionaire in America. Sharing some millionaires' life stories with you is essential to your journey to becoming successful like us. In chapter one, you'll find great stories about some successful immigrants.

Chapter 1

Be a Millionaire

Most of the millionaires are some ordinary people -- like you -- who start from scratch and become Rich. But it's crucial to know the principles and adhere to them for that to happen. To be a millionaire does not mean that you need to be a perfect person. As we all well know, no one is perfect. But you need to follow some important principles such as acquiring some knowledge of what you are doing, love what you are doing, and have control over what you are doing. When we read the story of certain millionaires in America, they are no better than you. The only difference is the fact that they have a purpose; they are focused, they devote themselves to the matter at hand, and they follow some principles. This book is essentially designed to teach you step-by-step in each chapter how to get there.

When I came to the United to pursue my dream, I had no family living here. I had to stay in a family friend's house for sometime. As a visitor who had no legal status to stay in the country no more than six months with no work permit from immigration, it was very difficult for me to find a job and support myself. I settled in Atlanta, Georgia where I got my first job with a manufacturing company to clean some production machines that they used to prepare vegetables for distribution. The only thing I could do at that moment was simply live like a survivor. As the only opportunity life offered at that time, I managed to save every dime that I could save and lived as simply as possible. While working for a minimum wage with that manufacturing company, I was anxious to learn the American culture. Not too long after, I found out that America's population reflects remarkable ethnic diversity. I believed if I knew the culture, I would be part of the American value that will eventually open all doors of opportunities for me so I could achieve the American Dream because I also knew that the American people have been trained since very early in their lives to consider themselves as separate individuals who are responsible for their own situations in life and their own destinies. I pressed on, eager to be among those successful people in America. It was a dream come true!

Herjavec Robert successful story

Herjavec was born in Yugoslavia and emigrated with his mother and father to Canada at the age of eight, after escaping communism in former Yugoslavia. Herjavec's father was incarcerated for speaking out against Marshal Josip Broz Tito's communist regime. Herjavec has become well known for his family's "rags to riches" story of success, arriving with a single suitcase. The Herjavec family arrived in Halifax, Nova Scotia aboard the Cristoforo Colombo in 1970. The family eventually settled in Toronto where they lived in the basement apartment of a family friend's home for 18 months.

Herjavec graduated from New College at the University of Toronto, with a degree in English literature and political science. To make a living and help support his family, the took on a variety of minimum wage jobs such as waiting tables, delivering newspapers and retail sales.

Herjavec's first career was in film at an early age. He quickly moved behind the camera in various production roles. He worked in several productions as a 3rd AD (assistant director) including Cain and Abel and The Return of Billy Jack. His early film career culminated with the position of Field Producer of the XIV Winter Olympic Games in Sarajevo, Bosnia and Hercegovina for Global TV – where he was given an honor as one of the youngest producers of Olympic coverage.

In between productions, Herjavec found himself looking for work. Through his roommate, he learned of an opening at a computer startup called Logiquest selling IBM mainframe emulation boards. He found himself under-qualified for the position but talked his way into the role by offering to work for free for the first six months to earn his stay. In order to pay the rent during this free period, Herjavec worked as waitress at a restaurant at night in Yorkville. He eventually ended up as General Manager of Logiquest. In 1990, he left to found BRAK Systems, a Canadian integrator of Internet security software, from the basement of his home. BRAK Systems was sold to AT&T Canada in 2000.

After a three-year retirement as a stay-at-home father to his three children, Herjavec founded the Herjavec Group in 2003, a security solutions integrator, reseller and managed service provider, of which he is currently the CEO. The Herjavec Group is one of Canada's fastest-growing technology companies and the country's largest IT security provider, according to the Branham Group, The Herjavec Group (THG) has grown from three employees in 2003 to 150 employees as of 2013, with a 643% growth rate from 2007–2012 and sales from $400K in 2003 to over $125 million in 2012. The company has done over $500 million in sales in the last 10 years. Herjavec and the Herjavec Group Inc. have been the recipients of numerous entrepreneurial and business achievement awards.

Robert demonstrates his entrepreneurial expertise through his leading role on the Emmy nominated, hit American TV show, Shark Tank, now in its 5th season on ABC (produced by Mark Burnett Productions). His inspiring books, .Driven. and .The Will to Win., were simultaneously Top 10 Bestsellers that earned him the title of .Best Selling Author.. Robert's motivational business advice has received millions of impressions through TV, print, radio and digital media.

Tom Pendleton successful story

Tom Pendleton was born in Scotland and came to the United States in 1973. He spent many years working in the sign and display business after coming to the United States, making such things as the neon signs for beer companies seen in bars and restaurants. But a few years ago, he had an idea, researched whether it was a viable business and came up with a product line, leading to the creation of an international company now doing business on three continents. "I noticed that there wasn't too many safety products, especially for adults or the police or the emergency services, that had reflective vests that would actually light up," Pendleton says. With his background experience with LEDs and accessories, "I thought these folks should all be wearing LED vests."

"We came up with a whole bunch of safety products that we thought were very practical and unique and which should serve the consumer or emergency care for commercial companies preaching safety," he says. In 2006, Pendleton and his wife started SafetyBright.com with their savings, offering safety products designed to increase visibility for consumers as well as law enforcement and emergency responders.

Through his contacts and friends abroad, the company has been able to expand from the U.S. to Europe and Asia. A friend in the U.K. with a print design business has taken over running European operations. Pendleton, through an old connection in Hong Kong, was able to import some products made in China. Pendleton says starting a business in the U.S. was definitely easier than the U.K., due to the extensive paperwork and bureaucracy there. But perseverance still was key when starting the business, he says.

"I knew it was going to take three to five years for the business to take off and become fully profitable," Pendleton says. "I knew that I would have to invest and it took lots of time and energy with little reward for the first several years. My wife and I were willing to do that."

Miguel Zabludovsky successful story

Miguel Zabludovsky was born in Mexico and immigrated to the United Stated in 2000. He moved to New York for a girl after graduating from Boston University in 2004. The girl didn't last, but Zabludovsky entered another relationship -- a student-mentor relationship with a former professor who gave him the courage to open his own business.

At 29, Zabludovsky is the founder of Slate NYC, an eco-friendly and affordable laundry, dry cleaning and home cleaning service. The 4-year-old company is used by more than 5,000 customers in New York. Zabludovsky's father owned a detergent company that exposed him to the laundry business, but he only saw possibilities in the U.S. one day while dropping off his own clothes to be cleaned.

"The whole experience was a complete disaster," he says. "You take it to these dirty places. The wash-and-fold is not what you're expecting as a consumer. From the start there was an appearance issue, there was no customer service, the prices were all over the board." "I wanted a place that would pick up my stuff every Monday ... and charge me a monthly price. And I wanted to have my clothes cleaned with nontoxic chemicals," he says.

Zabludovsky drew up a business plan and began by shuffling around clothes to contracted dry cleaners. He finally built his own dry cleaning facilities in 2007 and started cleaning clothes. "Four years later we're one of the top five dry cleaners in New York and possibly the top three in terms of quality," he says. Last year, Slate NYC brought $1.2 million in revenue -- nearly five times the industry average.

Slate NYC wasn't immune to the recession. To diversify, Zabludovsky started a maid service and supplemented revenue lost from people who weren't dry cleaning as much. "Home cleaning is like dry cleaning: It's very fragmented. We felt that we could do a good job there as well, and tried that with the delivery of clothes," he says.

Access to capital was an issue. Slate NYC was originally financed through Zabludovsky's savings and contributions from family. In moving to Brooklyn to a larger space, Zabludovsky says, he was turned down for a U.S. Small Business Administration loan, even backed by collateral, because he wasn't a U.S. citizen. He ended up going to a specialized lender to fund his expansion. On a positive note, Zabludovsky said having Mexican roots helped him hire for the company's 25 full-time employees. "I'm Mexican. I speak Spanish. I can find really good people to work for us," he says.

Zabludovsky says having a mentor, whom he describes as a "shrewd Turkish businessman," was important. Starting a business "is very emotional, but if you have someone who can coach you emotionally and has the experience -- that for me was a huge advantage," he says.

Bhuvana Krishnan successful story

Bhuvana Krishnan was born in India and came to the United States in 1998. He graduated college with degrees in electrical engineering in India at the height of the Internet bubble and ended up getting a job in computer programming. She came to the U.S. on a work project at the Nasdaq in 1998 for what was supposed to be three months, "but then they needed me on another project," she says. "One thing led to another and then met my husband and stayed here," she says. "This became home." Krishnan went back to school, got her MBA, moved to Georgia and slowly gathered the courage to fulfill a long-term dream of opening her own business.

"As an Indian, entrepreneurship runs in our blood, but the environment in India was just not conducive to that," she says. "America is the land of opportunity. If you're good at something, you can make it here. While in India there is just so much bureaucratic stuff to overcome ... particularly as a woman. I couldn't have done it entirely on my own as I can here."

Cybertary is a nationwide franchise network of virtual assistants providing services to business owners. "At some point in their business, they need help -- and they need skilled help -- and that's where we come in," according to Krishnan, the owner of Cybertary's Alpharetta, Ga., franchise. Cybertary is a "team of professionals that can provide these services on a demand basis."

Krishnan contemplated starting a business along similar lines as Cybertary for several years. She had the intention of setting up the business while still working full-time at an insurance company "and that just didn't happen," she says.

Through a friend, Krishnan was introduced to the Cybertary franchise network and chose in late 2009 to open a franchise because "my time to market would be drastically reduced" and she'd have support on the back end if needed, she says.

"I quit my job and started this at the height of the recession," she says. "It was definitely a big risk, but one that I haven't regretted."

As an immigrant business owner, Krishnan wishes she had grown up in the U.S. to learn the culture and history better, but she doesn't seem to have a problem getting clients. Like Zabludovsky, Krishnan says she has an advantage in being a minority: relating to the local Indian community. And people from other minority groups also tend to gravitate to her.

"They feel more comfortable talking to me. They feel like I understand it as an immigrant," she says. In her local community, "there is a huge Indian and Asian community ... I definitely have an advantage there." But she tries not to limit her network to the Indian community. Krishnan suggests that other business owners widen their comfort zone when it comes to getting clients and strengthening professional networks.

"Building relationships as an immigrant is by no means easy," she says. "Trying to build a business in a foreign land is not easy at all, but the more you go out and talk to people and network and the more you're seen in the community ... You will form more relationships and grow your business."

Lowell Hawthorne successful story

Lowell Hawthorne was born in Jamaica and came to America in 1981. He grew up in Jamaica, where his family owned a bakery business. It was the entrepreneurial spirit of his parents that stuck with him even after he came to America.

"Once I arrived, like most immigrants I had to find employment," he says. Hawthorne ended up being employed by the New York Police Department, eventually making his way to become an accountant within the NYPD's pension section.

After 10 years, he decided he wanted to bring (what his family did best) Jamaica to the U.S. He called a family meeting to gather support and got it; family members ended up taking out second mortgages on their homes to back the launch.

Golden Krust Caribbean Bakery & Grill opened its first establishment in the Bronx, N.Y. -- where there is a large Caribbean population -- in 1989, finding strong demand. Golden Krust opened 17 restaurants throughout the boroughs of New York City in just five years and became a franchised establishment by default in 1996, Hawthorne says. It has expanded to 125 franchised stores in nine states along the Eastern Seaboard.

Hawthorne says his success depended on serving its primary customer -- the Caribbean community. It also would not have succeeded if there was no family support. "There are seven of us family members, along with spouses, and each person brings a very unique skill to the organization. I was able to capitalize on those skills," Hawthorne says. In the beginning, for instance, Hawthorne's father would come from Jamaica to help bake. Hawthorne also says that to get the product to a quality he was used to in Jamaica, he ended up importing equipment, raw material and employees from Jamaica. Bringing employees to the U.S. was a whole new set of challenges, including having to secure work Visas. "It was very challenging, but like anything else we did what we had to do," he says. For an immigrant business owner, learning the rules and language of franchises wasn't easy.

"There was no school, no institution that one could have gone to learn the business. So I basically applied to various franchise organizations to learn about the franchise business and tried to get the best attorneys on board and best accountants on board," Hawthorne says. "There was a whole lot to do and there were not many Caribbean businesses that were in the franchise business."

Golden Krust is expanding its reach by moving to the retail market and selling to the Costco chain, penal institutions and institutional accounts, Hawthorne says. "It was not easy putting it together, but we did it," Hawthorne says. "It was worth it to the very end."

Yuri Schneiberg successful story

Yuri Schneiberg came to the U.S. from St. Petersburg in Russia in 1979 with strong computer programming skills and a desire to use those skills in education. He and his wife originally ran a computer programming school with two campuses, serving 1,500 students, but sold it in 1997. Shortly after, they shifted the client list from consumer to commercial clients and started Learnquest, which provides vocational training in IT and other business disciplines to Fortune 1000 businesses and government agencies.

The company operates training sessions all over the country and virtually, and has five regional sales offices across the U.S. and one in Canada.

This September, Schneiberg will be adding to LearnQuest's offerings by launching The Entrepreneurship and Small Business Management certificate program. It was the recession that sparked the idea.

"As unemployment continues to be high, and we have 25 years of experience, we would like to offer some help to our peers in small business," he said. "We want to share our experience with other small-business owners, including immigrants. This is definitely one of our target audiences. As an immigrant and small-business owner with an MBA -- his son has one as well -- Schneiberg says his practical experience will help others who are starting out.

"Those who would benefit the most would be the people who've been in business for a year, got a taste, and what they learned is what they don't know. They're ready to take off, ready to start hiring," he says. "Our program will put them in the right position, where the growth is not already a mile ahead of them."

Mark Cuban successful story

Born in Pittsburgh, Pennsylvania, Mark Cuban has always been a sports enthusiastic and sports fanatic. At the age of 12, he was selling garbage bags with the only purpose to buy a new pair of high end basketball sneakers. However, this dealing sowed the seeds of business dealing to come. Throughout his high school, he continued to work anything like promoting disco parties and bar-tending.

Mark Cuban is one of the exceptionally successful American entrepreneurs who has a net worth of $2.6 Billion according to Forbes. Popularly known as "Shark Tank," he lives a life that most people envy. He founded his first company called Micro Solutions and sold it for $6-million to CompuServe in 1995. But this was just the knack of his real success, he had a long way to go.

The very same year, Cuban started a new company, Audionet, which eventually turned into Broadcast.com. The main idea was based on webcasting, to put live sporting events online for anyone to listen to. By 1999, Cuban grew the company to the team of over 300 employees and made $100 million in annual revenues during the dot com boom.

He ended up becoming a billionaire, when Yahoo picked Broadcast.com for $5.9 Billion just before the dot com crash. So, whether you called it a plain luck or his prediction, he won the poker game of his life.

After completing his graduation from Indiana University, he got his first job in the early 80's in a software company named, Your Business Software. During his time with the company, PC's were growing swiftly and he made a handsome relationships with multiple software clients. He started meeting clients on the side to seek the business opportunity to grow his own business. Seeing this, the Company fired him but his clients came with him.

Founded MicroSolutions

After getting fired from his job, Cuban launched his own company named, MicroSolutions, without wasting any time. The company was based on software reselling which gained a lot of publicity in a very short time. A few years later, in 1990, Cuban sold MicroSolutions to CompuServe for $6 million. After clearing all the taxes, Cuban ended up with $2 million in his pocket. In the mid 90's he was busy trading in stocks. He became the investor and at that point, Cuban had turned his $2 million into $20 million.

His passion for Sports turved into a huge profitable business. In 1998, along with his college friend, Cuban started another company named, Audionet.com. Both were huge fans of basketball, their business was online portal merging basketball and webcasting. Later on, he changed the company's name to Broadcast.com. The Broadcast.com expanded to over 300 employees and $100 million in annual revenue by late 90's.

When dot com was booming, he decided to sell Broadcast.com to Yahoo. Finally, in 1999, Yahoo picked it up for $5.9 BILLION in Yahoo stock. When the deal was officially closed, it was the peak time of dot com and Yahoo's stock was trading at $163 per share.

After six months, when he had full access to his stock shares, he gambled all his shares and dumped his entire stake on the open market. Within a week, he sold every single share of Yahoo and was left with $2.5 BILLION in cash to his side.

And the most interesting part is, the share that he sold for nearly $160 crashed within the next 18 months to $8.11 PER SHARE.

Today he owns a basketball team--Dallas Mavericks, Landmark Theaters, film distribution company- Magnolia Pictures, 24,000 square foot mansion in Dallas and a private jet worth $40 million.

Andrew Carnegie successful story

Andrew Carnegie was born into a typical lower-class family in Scotland, and lived in a weavers cottage; a very small house. The main room served not only as the living quarters but also the dining room as well as the bedroom for the family. His family were suffering from near starvation and poverty when William, his father, emigrated the family to Allegheny, Pennsylvania in the USA. The area in which they lived was very poor but better than their previous community in Fife. The first job he had was that of a bobbin boy where he helped change spools for 12hrs each day. Feeling this wasn't the career for him he went on to become a telegraph messenger for $2.50 per week; his job came with a couple of perks too, such as gaining free entry to the local theatre. He soon progressed to $4.00 per week when he was 18 yrs old, and through hard work rapidly development and Andrew climbed swiftly through the ranks. Eventually he became an investor, investing the money he had saved over the years into Adams Express Company, a messenger service.

Carnegie later received shares in a car business after helping to safeguard the shares of another business for a friend; he used this to his advantage and reinvested all his money into the railway industry. During the civil war Carnegie made a fortune through investments he had made; one of which had him investing $40,000 of his own money into Story Farm; a creek rich in oil. By the end of the year, the investment had paid of in dividends to the tidy sum of $1 million, as well as more profits coming in from the petrol and oil goods. After the Civil War had ended, Carnegie gave $40,000 to help build a library in his native Dunfermline, he also gave $50,000 of his money to a hospital college to help teach more nurses and save more lives. Now an investor in both oil and steel Carnegie was becoming very wealthy, and decided to write his first book which sold over 40,000 copies. His writing style and intelligence helped Carnegie become known as a great author and journalist which helped him earn another hefty fortune in doing so. By 1898 Carnegie was worth more than $20 million and famously offered $20,000,000 to buy the Philippines from Spain in a bid to allow them independence. By the time of his death in 1919, Carnegie had become famous for his investments, his oil, his writings and, of course, his entrepreneurial streak. With the money he made from all his investments he died a very wealthy man, his net worth being $350,695,653, today that figure would be nearly $300 billion.

At some point, most people have said to themselves they want to be like one of the people in this list, "I want to be the next Paul J. Toyle, Bhuvana Krishnan, Miguel Zabludovsky, Herjavec

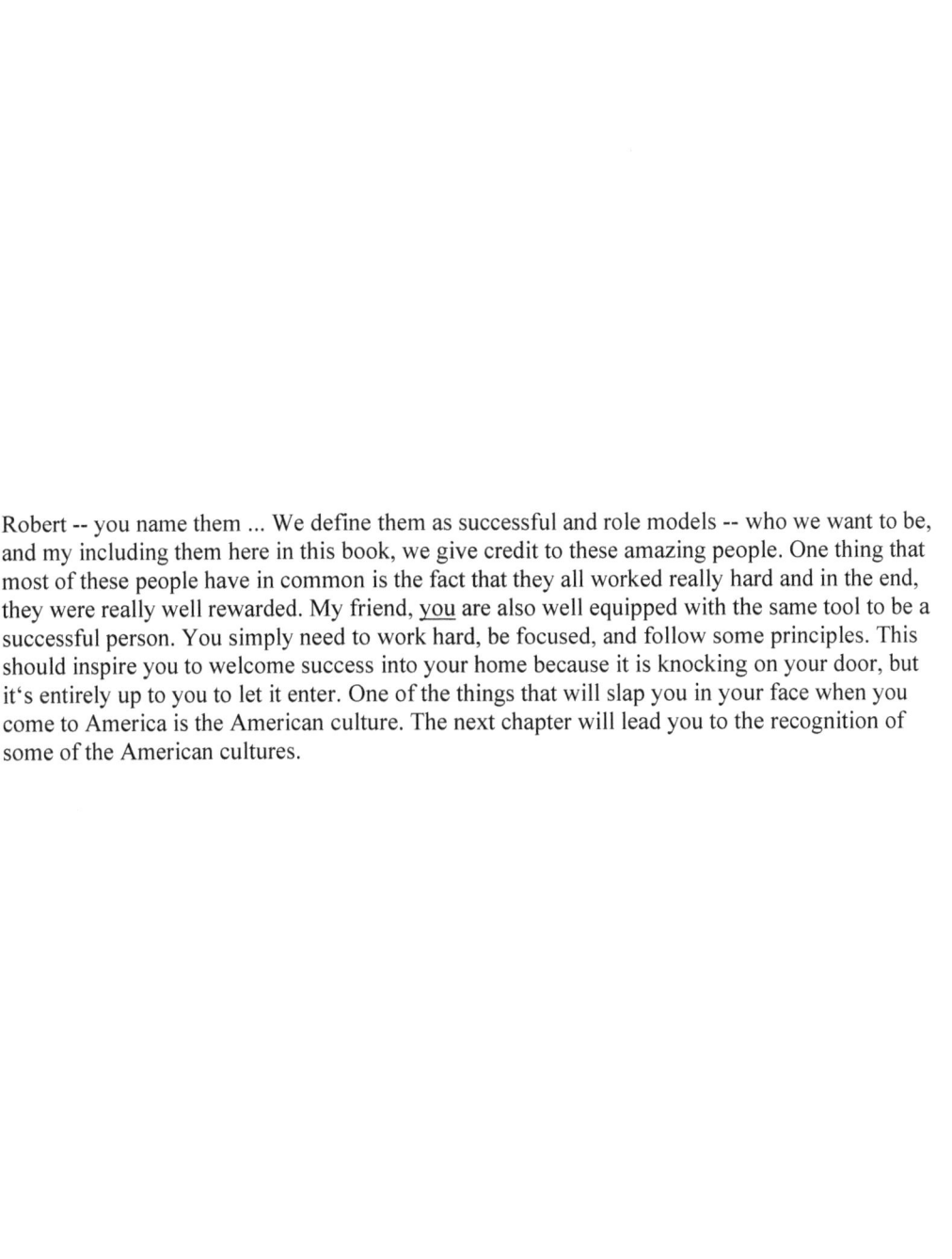

Robert -- you name them ... We define them as successful and role models -- who we want to be, and my including them here in this book, we give credit to these amazing people. One thing that most of these people have in common is the fact that they all worked really hard and in the end, they were really well rewarded. My friend, <u>you</u> are also well equipped with the same tool to be a successful person. You simply need to work hard, be focused, and follow some principles. This should inspire you to welcome success into your home because it is knocking on your door, but it's entirely up to you to let it enter. One of the things that will slap you in your face when you come to America is the American culture. The next chapter will lead you to the recognition of some of the American cultures.

Chapter 2

Cross Cultural

Don't be caught in an old culture

It's important to be open-minded when it comes to cross culture in achieving your goal. Adjusting to a new culture can be a time of experiencing new customs, values, and beliefs, as you are literally immersed in a new culture and possibly a new language, as well. It can also be a time of confusion as you try to learn how to respond appropriately to cues that can seem foreign, and to "do the right thing" culturally. Many people are so confused, some wonder if they will ever pass that stage. To them, they compare their lives with a car that turns upside down while they are still inside of it and struggling to get out. My answer to you, you will eventually get out of the car but you need to be patient and tenacious. The harder you try, the faster you will get out of it. Avoid putting too much pressure on yourself but let it flow with simply your tenacity. Remember, it's a new life and a lot to learn in that process. People have different speeds and levels of learning, and so many different reasons but you can adjust your speed of learning over time.

American value

People may not respond the way they did back home. Contrary to the facial behavior promoted by certain cultures, other groups provide an upbringing which may increase the likelihood of teacher-student conflict. For example, in the Hispanic culture, which tends to be male dominant, adolescent boys may resist complying with commands from female educators. With these students, cooperation is best gained through non- authoritative methods which "request" rather than demand compliance.

While touch is often recommended as a reinforcement procedure, especially for cultural groups that use a great deal of bodily contact, it may be contra-indicated for some Asian students. Those whose heritage was influenced by Confusionism view the body as being more sacred as one approaches the area of the head where the soul is believed to reside As an example of culturally disrespectful intervention, consider that in the majority of American culture, a child is expected to look at the authority figure when being disciplined. Lowered eyes are associated with deceit or inattention. To gain eye contact, the instructor may lift the student's chin and say "Look at me when I'm talking to you." The educator may not realize that in many Asian, Black, and Hispanic homes, children are taught to lower their eyes when being disciplined as a sign of respect, and other behavior management systems that recommend gaining eye contact while disciplining, unknowingly fail to respect the behavior promoted in the student's home environment. Additionally, the teacher probably fails to realize that direct eye contact by these students during disciplinary situations typically indicates defiance rather than respect. The educator may also not realize that many culturally diverse children smile during disciplinary situations, not to express defiance, but rather due to anxiety, appeasement attempts or confusion as to why the instructor is confronting them. Behavioral patterns and actions considered to be abnormal vary by culture. When educators and their charges come from different backgrounds, it can be expected that each will often display behaviors different than those in the other's culture.

This country was founded on the rugged individualism of the earlier pioneers and settlers, many of whom came from Europe, and as a culture we still value this. Families tend to be less interdependent or close knit than in many societies.

There is a great deal of freedom of individual expression (and opinion) in this country, including religious belief that is tolerated as long as no one is bothered and people are respectful of one another. Open discussion of different beliefs and practices, and questioning our own beliefs and why we do things is common, especially within the youth in this country. Sometimes newcomers to our country are surprised at the number of rules and regulations that govern daily life, from how to cross a street to whether they can smoke in a public restaurant.

Learning these rules can take time.
Also certain cultural values such as discussion of sexuality, how women (and men!) dress, and program ratings in movies and on public television may be very different from your native country. To make things even more complicated, there are many different ethnic and cultural groups that make up our population, and standards may vary; some depending on which group you are with! It's important to listen and learn how things are done here, to ask questions when you aren't sure, and to be patient with yourself as you learn what is acceptable and not in this new culture.

People in our culture tend to be direct, and to speak what they are thinking or feeling more than in some cultures, and this is considered okay. Being frank and honest (but not cruelly blunt) is considered a good thing. People also enjoy debating issues in a friendly manner, and exchanging ideas. Sometimes American behavior may seem rude to you because we are more outspoken, but usually the comments are well intentioned and not meant to be disrespectful.

Many Americans are forward thinking, and believe that a person can control their own destiny by working hard and planning for the future. They also value their time (especially private time) and feel that "time is money". They admire people who show up to work early or on time, and who manage their time well.

We are a mobile culture, and people will move if their job depends on it. Some families move once every few years because of their work or other factors. And military families will move quite a bit, since they are stationed at new bases from time to time.

American school

School in America may begin with preschool (at age 3) or kindergarten (age 5), although it is not uncommon for young children under age 3 to be in childcare or daycare if both parents work and there are no grandparents who live nearby to help with this task. By the time children reach the age of five, they have learned a great deal. They have reached maturity by mastering their own language, having relationships with friends and family, and how they understand and react to familiar situations. Poor and minority children might meet the typical educational requirements for their home and other surroundings, but when placed in school, it is a lot harder for these children to adapt to the school atmosphere. When the children enter school, the teachers assume these qualifications have already been met. This is a huge problem because certain children from different cultural backgrounds might not be as well equipped with this information. This is where the community fits in. The children need to be ready for all aspects of school. School readiness can be increased by a higher quality preschool education and day care. Children should come to school ready to learn. If they fit into their families and communities, then we know that they are good learners. We only need to worry about the small minority of children who have handicapping conditions, or who live in extremely hazardous environments and, therefore, have not learned what their community teaches.

When a child's previous knowledge and skills do not prepare him for a new setting, like school, it is extremely hard. A child may be developed in their home environment, but yet unable to adapt easily to a school environment or succeed at the academic tasks valued by teachers. Children become what they live. Cultural patterns of interaction guide the growing child, but they also become the root for their definitions of themselves. When adults and children do not share common experiences or hold common beliefs about the meaning of experience, they are quick to misunderstand cultural interchanges (Bowman, 1989). Some teachers do not appreciate the real similarities and differences between their understanding of the world and that of children and families who come from different backgrounds. That is why we need to further educate the teachers in America. Most teachers in the United States come from a rural background and don't understand the learning habits of minority students. We need to hire teachers with experience in cultural studies.

Standardized testing of young children demonstrates the danger of using white, middle-class children as the gauge for judging other children. It is not a coincidence that poor and minority children are common in certain types of special education and at-risk programs. Standardized tests do not separate culture from development. The child may know something else that is equal in knowledge, but if he or she does not know what is on the test, we assume that there is something wrong.

Some minorities just simply won't make any effort toward the schooling system. Mostly African Americans, Hispanic, and Native Americans are the minorities that this applies to. These groups are more likely to avoid learning skills associated with the white middle class since their efforts will not pay off with the same opportunities that the other students will obtain (Ogbu, 1992). Consequently, they develop a poor education. The preschool and primary years are critical ones if children are to be successful in school, and we must carefully review the treatment of children during these years. School readiness can be increased by higher quality preschool education and day care (Kagan, 1991). One way of making a difference would be to change how schools interact with other community organizations. Relationships with social services, parks, libraries, day care centers, and homes are very important when it comes to the minorities' education. Any school that is not making a relationship with these organizations cannot seriously claim to be focusing on educational success for all. Another remedy to the situation is to listen to the voices of the minorities. It is very important that minority communities feel a better sense of ownership on school standards if they are to help in preparing their children (Kagan, 1991). Involvement by parents and community members from these minority groups is crucial for making a change. A last and final suggestion would be to further educate teachers and schools for a better understanding of the minority students. Teachers and the schools really need to get involved in all the different communities and community organizations. This would give the minorities a much better chance to succeed in the classroom and pursue their future education. The kind of change we want to have accomplished is not easy. It will require a lot of skill and effort from all of us if it is to happen. Unless we speak out about the relationship between culture, development, and education, we cannot hope to provide the kind of schooling needed to carry us safely into the future.

American transportation

Transportation may be different because some countries don't have system transportation in place like here in the U.S. Many countries around the world overlook the rule and regulation of transportation. To recognize transportation culture, start by asking what are our accepted behaviors on roads? What have we agreed upon as uses of shared streets? A few books that consider how we got to where we are today in transportation culture are Peter Norton's *Fighting Traffic* and Clay McShane's *Down the Asphalt Path*. Can the street on its own transform the stories people tell each other about transportation if cultural norms are not taken into account? At dinner tables, over coffee — this is where people tell each other about the right ways to travel.

The way they interact in the street is an outgrowth of a larger mental framework they reinforce through buying bigger and bigger cars at the dealer, talking about bicyclists as a problem, confirming to each other that all the driving is a shame, but there is no alternative.

Those of us who bike know that's not the case. With our bodies on our bikes, we map what is possible. We make visible the lines between home, work, shopping, and fun. And in bike shops, co-ops, on rides, in all the places where people talk and wrench and race, bicycling is normal. Spending time in these spaces fuels us and gives us the vocabulary to go tell others about what a great thing biking can be.

The investment in public transportation by the federal government has paid off with new rail and rapid bus transit lines or extensions that have opened up in recent years. These new services have not only created greater access for people to use public transit, but have led to economic development that has transformed and revitalized the community. Public transportation is not just moving people, but also positively shaping the communities we live in

American music

Many newcomers greatly enjoy American music. Music has always been a part of American culture. In 19th-century America, ragtime was a national craze, music was taught in schools, and households had 5 million pianos. After the Industrial Revolution, a musical culture emerged that incorporated a variety of "root genres," from jazz and Latin to country western and bluegrass to folk and gospel music. In the 20th century, those genres were brought together under the dominant aesthetic of the Blues. The blues came right up from the bowels of the American soul.

The Blues united all American root styles, and brought together diverse musicians, black and white, under one musical language. This embracing of the Blues issued a deep indictment of racial injustice, it exposed the irony of living in a deeply segregated nation in which performers from all regions and classes chose to express [themselves] through an Afro-rooted music.

The early 20th century was a golden era of experimentation, when musicians of all races were surprisingly free to play together and to borrow songs and techniques. Musical genres were only labeled so that the record companies could sell them.

After World War II, however, things changed. America became a country of highly educated, wealthier citizens who, thanks to the rise of the suburbs, were more segregated than ever. American music, long a bastion of racial integration and a celebration of regional diversity, lost out to the increasingly popular medium of television, which presented a "white bread" portrait of American life that came to dominate the popular imagination.

Turmoil in the 1960s finally severed Americans from their musical tradition. After the Soviets launched Sputnik, American schools pushed math and science over music and arts. Young people, caught up in political rebellion, developed their own musical traditions of rock and folk to break from what they saw as a corrupt past. Our music, genetically engineered to bring us together, became the principal tool for keeping us apart. After the Vietnam War ended, what remained were generations whose social, political, and musical agendas barely survived beyond satire, beyond commerce, beyond apathy..

Modern Americans can't appreciate a musical past that they don't know existed, Marsalis told the crowd. Indeed, a large part of his mission is to bring the importance of that shared past to life by sparking conversation not just among musicians but with leaders in education, business, and other fields. There are instructive lessons for America's cultural future that can only be found in knowing and embracing the root styles, and in mastering the regional and national particulars of our identity as sung by our greatest poets.

As time goes on.

American TV

TV is a constant presence in most Americans' lives. With its fast-moving, visually interesting, highly entertaining style, it commands many people's attention for several hours each day. Studies have shown that television competes with other sources of human interaction—such as family, friends, church, and school—in helping young people develop values and form ideas about the world around them. It also influences viewers' attitudes and beliefs about themselves, as well as about people from other social, ethnic, and cultural backgrounds.

Between the 1940s and 2000s, commercial television had a profound and wide-ranging impact on American society and culture. It influenced the way that people think about such important social issues as race, gender, and class. It played an important role in the political process, particularly in shaping national election campaigns. TV programs and commercials have also been mentioned as major factors contributing to increased American materialism (a view that places more value on acquiring material possessions than on developing in other ways). Finally, television helped to spread American culture around the world.

Racial minorities on TV

Until the 1970s, the majority of the people who appeared on American television programs were Caucasian (white). Being white was presented as normal in all sorts of programs, including news, sports, entertainment, and advertisements. The few minorities that did appear in TV programs tended to be presented as stereotypes (generalized, usually negative images of a group of people). For instance, African American actors often played roles as household servants, while Native Americans often appeared as warriors in Westerns.

Some critics argue that outright racism (unfair treatment of people because of their race) was the reason that so few minorities appeared on television. But television industry analysts offered several other explanations as well. In the 1950s and 1960s, for instance, the broadcast networks tried to create programs that would attract a wide audience. Before research tools became available to gather information about the race and gender of people watching, network programmers assumed that the audience was made up mostly of white viewers. They also assumed that many white viewers would not be interested in watching shows about minorities. In addition, the networks did not want to risk offending viewers—or potential advertisers—in the South who supported segregation (the forced separation of people by race). Whatever the reason, prime-time television programming largely ignored the real-life concerns and contributions of America's racial minorities for many years.

There were a few early TV shows that featured minorities. The popular situation comedy (sitcom) I Love Lucy, which aired from 1951 to 1957, co-starred comedian Lucille Ball (1911–1989) and her real-life husband, bandleader Desi Arnaz (1917–1986), who was Hispanic. The Nat "King" Cole Show, a musical variety series that began on NBC in 1956, was hosted by the well-known black entertainer Nat King Cole (1919–1965). Even though the program attracted many of the top performers of that time, it was cancelled after one year because it failed to find a sponsor (a company that pays to produce a program for advertising purposes). A very popular early variety program, The Ed Sullivan Show, featured a number of black performers as guests. Still, African Americans mostly appeared on TV in the role of entertainers.

This situation slowly began to improve during the civil rights movement (1965–75), when African Americans fought to end segregation and gain equal rights in American society. TV news programs provided extensive coverage of civil rights protests, which helped turn public opinion in favor of the cause of equality. As awareness of racial discrimination (unfair treatment based on race) increased, more social critics began complaining about the absence of minority characters on television. They argued that positive portrayals of minority characters in TV programs could help increase the self-esteem of minority viewers, promote understanding, and improve race relations in the United States.

During the 1970s, television program ratings began using such viewer characteristics as age, income, education, and ethnicity to break down the mass audience into smaller groups. Once the networks could collect more detailed data about the audience, they began creating programs to appeal to specific groups. Around this time, the networks also shifted their general focus away from older, rural viewers and toward younger, urban viewers, who were seen as more likely to spend money on sponsors' products. This change in audience focus led the networks to tackle more frequently debated issues in their programs.

As a result, several programs featuring minority characters and families first appeared in the 1970s. The African American comedian Flip Wilson (1933–1998) hosted a successful variety show that aired on NBC from 1970 to 1974. The Flip Wilson Show reached number two in the national TV rankings and won two Emmy Awards. Some historians credit Wilson for leading the way for later black comedians who had successful television careers, such as Arsenio Hall (1955–), Eddie Murphy (1961–), Chris Rock (1965–), and Dave Chappelle (1973–). However, other critics claim that Wilson started an unfortunate trend in which a growing number of African American entertainers on television played the role of comic fool.

American food

American cuisine has been influenced by Europeans and Native Americans in its early history. Today, there are a number of foods that are commonly identified as American, such as hamburgers, hot dogs, potato chips, macaroni-and-cheese, and meat loaf. "As American as apple pie" has come to mean something that is authentically American.

There are also styles of cooking and types of foods that are specific to a region. Southern-style cooking is often called "American comfort food" and includes dishes such as fried chicken, collard greens, black-eyed peas and corn bread. Tex-Mex, popular in Texas and the Southwest, is a blend of Spanish and Mexican cooking styles and includes items such as chili and burritos and relies heavily on shredded cheese and beans. Jerky, dried meats that are served as snacks, is also a food that was created in the United States, according to NPR

There are some arguments about our food system and its effect on life and health in America—arguments that hop from obesity to Type 2 diabetes to GMOs to food deserts to e-coli to high fructose corn syrup—that it's easy to miss a heartening truth, one we can be thankful for in this season of eating. The truth is that America is in the middle of inventing a new food culture, and no one, not the foodies nor the food activists nor the Grocery Manufacturers Association of America, can predict how powerful a force for change it may be. This food culture, spreading across the land like the bloom on a soft-ripened cheese, has the power to cure a lot of what ails us. Deep cultural change is the one force that can overcome generations of political and market inertia that has led to our overweight condition. A taste for better food could lift us from the adolescent excesses of our 20th century eating habits — and begin to reduce the obesity that has been the result.

American food culture in the last century swallowed the factory-to-table promise whole, a promise that seemed validated by the triumphs of nutrition science: Diet was perfectible for the shiny, fast-paced life that was God's destiny for Americans. Daily we would rise to vitamin-enriched spongy white breads and toaster pastries and powdered breakfast drinks; we would lunch on mass-manufactured hamburgers; we would snack on Hostess Twinkies; dine on huge steaks. We would replace water with soda, and make our beer taste like water. We would conquer the world on this high-octane fuel, in vast portions for our growing bodies. The anonymous food scientist was the de facto head chef of the nation. None of the factory foods, taken alone, was or is bad; taken together, though, and dominating our diet—turned out to be a different story.

The perfectible diet revealed its fatal flaws when chronic disease rates (first heart disease, much more recently Type 2 diabetes) rocketed and were linked as early as the 1950s to the supersized, supercharged, supersalted, superfatted foods we loved. But we would also awaken, slowly, to the limitations—in variety and in taste—of the food we ate. Newly prosperous Americans traveled and encountered deep food cultures abroad, in Europe, India, and Southeast Asia. Maybe pasta in cans wasn't the best pasta? Among the travelers were people like Alice Waters, who brought the real-food word home and insisted that a whole new story about American food was possible. The environmental movement blossomed, throwing light on problems with farming and fishing, and beginning to reconnect the idea that quality of food supply depends on quality of farming practices.

It takes time for values of, and stories about, authenticity, craftsmanship, heritage and flavor to fight their way through a system as shiny and robust as the American factory-to-table food culture. It takes decades to invent a new food culture. We are now 40 and 50 and 60 years past Alice Waters, Julia Child, Craig Claiborne and Rachel Carson. Do not let that turtle pace blind you to the acceleration of changes now underway. The variety of foods in any decent supermarket is astounding. Artisan food-making has become as cool as building apps for iPads. Young people are finding reasons to farm—and get involved in food activism—while farmers' markets are proliferating like zucchini. Chefs are rock stars, including countless local indie chefs who have no connection to Food Network Television.

The local/global groove that defines the emerging food culture—combining immigrant knowledge and older, regional American traditions with the mashup tastes of the Internet-nurtured young—is the dominant groove of the new eating. I care what happens in New York and San Francisco and Chicago and New Orleans, but I care more that those things are also happening in Atlanta, Miami, Minneapolis, Austin and both Portlands: Name your city. The new food culture is trans-demographic: Good things come from Korexican taco trucks as much as from the experimentations of Grant Achatz. Chefs like Andy Ricker of the Portland and Brooklyn Thai restaurants called Pok Pok: these folks are the coolest of all, as they dive deeper into what authenticity actually means in America. The emerging food culture is inclusive, too, revering the knowledge of the grey-hairs: Hipster chef David Chang worships self-described hillbilly Tennessee bacon god Allan Benton.

Food companies want to be, must be, tuned to this new food culture. They cannot thrive otherwise. Critics of the food system fail to recognize that Big Food cannot dictate tastes to a new generation any more than the backers of Pat Boone could determine which singer—Boone or Presley—would define the exploding music culture of the 50 years that followed. We have to hope that problems such as obesity will, over a generation or two, be ameliorated by a taste for better food in different proportions; let's hope so, because there is no emerging medical or legislative cure. I am not arguing that food activists should not bother with their fights for social justice in the food system: In this economy, in this country with its pockets of poverty and its food deserts, God bless them. But they should be comforted that bigger forces are with them, stronger winds are at their backs, than mere politics and lobbying. Culture itself is changing. Taste raises consciousness. Those of us who love food can only marvel and enjoy. The election may be over, but we vote with our forks thrice daily—not only in the holiday season, but every day of the year. With the holiday season approaching, it will be interesting to know how many Americans will be reaching for a new cookbook to plan their holiday feast or will add the latest Top Chef DVD-boxed set to their gift list. After all, Americans' love of food and cooking continues to undeniably expand. According to Nielsen BookScan, which compiles statistics for the publishing industry, sales of "cooking/entertainment" books have jumped 4 percent in the U.S. this year.

Although this indicates a rise in a "foodie culture," what does it say about American food culture? Does this mean that we have one?

In a recent article in TIME, writer Josh Ozersky awakened this debate with chefs from around the country by suggesting we have yet to declare our culinary independence. Perhaps that is true. But isn't America founded on beliefs brought from other societies? Even Henry Ford, as Chef Michael Schwartz of Michael's Genuine in Miami reminded us in response to the TIME article, admits, "I invented nothing new" I simply assembled into a car the discoveries of other men behind whom were centuries of work.

It could be argued that all food cultures—Italian, Greek, European, in general—were developed because of those who settled there and brought their culture with them. And, as they moved westward, more was learned and carried to the next spot. Ultimately, those influences landed in America, bringing with them a melting pot of flavors, ingredients, techniques and methods. Even Italian cuisine, with a rich culinary history that is traceable over the last 2000 years, was influenced by ancient Greek, ancient Roman, Jewish and Arab cuisines, which, in turn, influenced French Cuisine.

Many established cultures and traditions were drawn from what was obtainable and necessary for preservation. Even the first "American" meal, Thanksgiving, was full of English influence and presence, while indigenous ingredients—native birds and game, fish and shellfish, herbs, nuts, plums, melons, grapes, cranberries, leeks, wild onions, beans, Jerusalem artichokes, squash—were used because of access and availability.

Since that first Thanksgiving in 1621, we have been introduced to ingredients and flavors that we never could have known without modern travel opportunities and storage capabilities. Today, there are few ingredients that we cannot access or experience. This is evidenced across the U.S. on restaurant menus both on the independent front and at the chain level.

Although there is doubt in the establishment of a "food culture," the reality is that American cuisine is very present on the menu. Mintel Menu Insights recently published their Top 10 Cuisine Types on Restaurant Menus featuring Traditional American at the top of the list—a 27% increase from Q2 2008–Q2 2011. American Regional Cuisine was also included with Southwestern and BBQ. And the reality is that when ordering Italian, Mexican and Chinese from the menu, consumers are most often experiencing Americanized versions of these cuisines. As we look to 2012, we can expect Asian influence to be more present than ever through modern takes on Thai cuisine and the growing occurrence of Indian street food on the menu.

Perhaps more than ever, our "food culture" can be captured by the recognition of a mindset that is driving our dining decisions. For example, in a recent panel discussion with a Midwestern American college-aged group, the question was posed, "What does one week of meals look like for you?" The response received was indicative of the options surrounding American consumers on a daily basis. With her eyes searching the ceiling as she recounted her week, she responded, "Halal, Mexican, Chinese, Italian/Pasta, Corn Dogs." Expansive choice is just the American way.

In comparison to the established cultures of European and Asian societies, America is just getting started. With the growing interest in food and cooking as a consumer passion, we just might be starting to develop the path to recognition. Author Christopher Powell, a contributor to the launch of Williams-Sonoma, was quoted recently by The Christian Science Monitor as saying, "Food has become an entire lifestyle. It's no longer just about preparation or consumption."

While that path continues to be paved, we'll remain content with the bounties of the melting pot, knowing that America's culinary landscape was founded initially in our independence to explore. We'll continue taking pride in blazing new trails, putting an unexpected spin on the expected and making something irrefutably ours. Imagination, creativity, experimentation, and limitless expression are all at the very core of the busiest restaurants around the country (including the rise of the gourmet food truck). This path to self-discovery is certainly one that's worthy of celebration, and consumers will continue to get in line to experience the results.

America is overlooking the real cause of its ever-expanding waistline, said Kelly Brownell, PhD, at APA's 2001 Annual Convention. The problem isn't so much people's lack of self-control, he said. It's a "toxic food environment"—the strips of fast-food restaurants along America's roadways, the barrage of burger advertising on television and the rows of candies at the checkout counter of any given convenience store.

"Whoever thought you could go eat at a gas station?" said Brownell, a Yale University psychology professor, adding that, with a new concept being test-marketed, "While you're pumping your gas you punch in the Fritos, the Twinkies and the Coke, and somebody brings it to your car. So the physical activity required to go in and get it is eliminated."

To be sure, Brownell acknowledged, genes and self-control play a role in obesity and diabetes and other health problems that result. But, in his view, both face a losing battle against the ubiquity of bad food. The problem with medical and psychological interventions for individuals, he said, is that the costs of treatment outweigh the benefits, and weight-gain relapse rates remain high. What's needed instead, he said, are broader-scale policy fixes that promote healthier foods and behaviors across American society.

"It's important for us to look at this from a public health point-of-view, where we're not so concerned with how overweight an individual is, but how overweight the population is," said Brownell. "Genetics is what permits the problem to occur, but environment is what drives it."

Of particular concern to Brownell is America's passive acceptance of unhealthy food. Americans fail to recognize, for example, the possible damage done by such fast-food icons as Ronald McDonald. "We take Joe Camel off the billboard because it is marketing bad products to our children, but Ronald McDonald is considered cute," said Brownell. "How different are they in their impact, in what they're trying to get kids to do?"

Certain "toxic signs" alarm Brownell:

As further evidence that environment is to blame, Brownell noted that obesity has risen notably in other countries, including China, and that migrants to Western countries have much higher obesity rates than their relatives back home.

Particularly vulnerable to the problem are American children, said Brownell. Soda companies and fast-food outlets increasingly ink contracts with schools and gear advertising to kids. "The most intrepid parents can't win this fight," he said.

In a new culture, the adjustment that we have to make is enormous and stressful. Many people dealing with these new stressors feel some anxiety, which is normal and has been called "culture shock".

The symptoms of culture shock will be different for each person, and can include feeling lonely or mildly depressed. Feeling stressed or irritable, and wanting to isolate from others are other common symptoms. You may feel overwhelmed trying to absorb all of the new aspects of living in this country. At times you may feel homesick and think longingly about your native country. You may even feel unsure of yourself as you try to figure out how things are done here. But it's a process that every immigrant has to go through. The road is not straight forward but it's shorter than you think. A great state of mind can help you overcome this challenge unexpectedly because it's not far from getting over with.

There are stages to adjusting to a new culture which are normal and that most people pass through (it doesn't last forever, it just feels that way at times). These include:
Everything is Just Great. This is the wonderful "honeymoon phase" when everything looks wonderful and the newness of the new country is exciting and pleasant. You may feel excited about being here, and the new opportunities that are waiting for you. When you go to the stores and visit, you may be impressed by how big everything is, and by how things are done here. If people ask you questions, you will smile.

Hostility

Problems may start occurring because of language and communication difficulties, or because of differences between your native culture and those here in the United States. At this point, you may start to feel impatient, irritable, frustrated, anxious, sad, or discontent, and to think that this new country may not be so wonderful after all. Americans may seem abrupt, rude, or too different from the people from your native land, and our culture may seem a mass of new rules that are difficult to learn. You may also feel homesick for your home country.

Understanding

At this stage, you will begin to feel more "at home' and able to get around, both physically, with the language, and emotionally. Things are starting to make sense now, and you don't feel as lost or bewildered by the way things are done here. At this point many people start comparing their old culture with our new one, and deciding which practices seem better. You start to regain your sense of humor, and you may even laugh at some of the misunderstandings that you have had. At this point, you will have a better understanding of our culture and realize that it is neither all good or all bad. You also start to feel that you "belong here". You will have accepted America as your home, and have learned to adjust to the differences in culture here.

People progress through these stages at their own rate. Some will last longer than others, and you will respond uniquely based on your own personality and methods of coping with new experiences. Interestingly enough, after going through all of these stages, if a person then goes back to live in their country of birth, they may go through a "re-entry shock" and need to go through them all over again!

Tips for Helping the Adjustment

It's important to be patient with yourself while adjusting to a new culture and to learn to utilize resources available to help you, whether a language class or local ethnic community group which can give a refreshing language and culture break and help lessen loneliness as you adjust to the country. You may have had some preconceptions about our culture, based on reading books, watching American films, or talking to others who have been to the United States. While some of the ideas of American life may be accurate, others may be exaggerated or unrealistic, and you may feel quite a bit of surprise as you learn the reality of living here.

What I learn about America

I realize that these feelings are normal. Everyone who comes to a new country and culture goes through them to some extent, a sense of humor helps. Sometimes the differences between cultures, or situations that can come up, are humorous and can help with releasing some of your feelings as you adjust to new ways of doing things. Look at some of the differences between your expectations of your new country, and the reality. You may have thought Americans acted one way, or that our country was a certain way, and then found out that things are actually quite different here. Realizing that the two might be quite different can help with adjusting to the reality of life here.Try to put yourself in the other place. Imagine what it would be like for your new American friends if they were suddenly placed in your culture. This can help you be a little more open minded, and empathetic to the differences. Get involved with others: whether with a hobby, a team sport, or other activity, doing things with others will help you with both your English acquisition, and with the feelings of loneliness that can occur. Mutual interests are a great way to make new friends, so consider taking that art class, or volunteering in a local community

Take good care of yourself by eating nutritiously and getting plenty of rest. Exercise, especially group sports or even walking with another person, can help with stress reduction and help ease some of the loneliness at the same time. Share how you feel with family or close friends. The support of others can help as you adjust to our culture and also grieve the loss of close contact with friends or family in your native land. Making new friends at work or school can also help with learning to accept your new culture and language. Set realistic goals for yourself, even if it's learning the bus route to your work by the end of the week, or learning seven new words in English over the next five days. This can help build-up your confidence as you see yourself reaching toward and achieving new things in your life.

American culture encompasses the customs and traditions of the United States. Culture encompasses religion, food, what we wear, how we wear it, our language, marriage, music, what we believe is right or wrong, how we sit at the table, how we greet visitors, how we behave with loved ones, and a million other things. The next chapter will open up with one of the most important elements in the America culture that basically keeps people morally together to the road of success, which is "religion."

Chapter 3

Religion in America

Nearly every known religion is practiced in the United States, which was founded on the basis of religious freedom. About 83 percent of Americans identify themselves as Christians, according to an ABC poll, while 13 percent replied that they had no religion at all. Another poll in 2012 reported similar findings. It also found that Judaism is the second most-identified religious affiliation, at about 1.7 percent of the population. Only 0.6 percent of respondents identified as Muslim. Many people view religion as a catalyst to success. According to a statistic, many religious people who face many life challenges find a great relief in the practice of their religion. Churches become more than a place for people to practice their religion faith but also a place that people find love, hope, renew and re-energize themselves to continue their daily life routine. The fact that they have a special place to refuel themselves after being hit by all kinds of life circumstances, they are resilient to stand firm in the midst of any crisis or start a new life. That's why the suicidal rate among religious people is at the lowest worldwide. No matter who you are, you may face some real challenges in your life, but someone needs to be prepared in case you face all kinds of occurrences. Because when the storm strikes, it may leave some people

dead, some paralyzed and others stranded. For the bible says, "Those the LORD blesses will inherit the land, but those he curses will be destroyed. The LORD makes firm the steps of the one who delights in him; though he may stumble, he will not fall, for the LORD upholds him with his hand. I was young and now I am old, yet I have never seen the righteous forsaken or their children begging bread. They are always generous and lend freely; their children will be a blessing." (Psalm 37:22-26) As the result, the Christian people are not alone in their battle because they have a Supreme Being who is watching over them and looking out for them.

It's not always happened that every attempt you make toward your goal is going to be successful. You may suffer minor loss or even great loss in that process. We have seen people react in different ways in different situations. Some are very resilient while others are so emotional that they are not even able to handle the least amount of uncertainty. Although we might experience some setbacks, we can't be pessimistic enough not to promptly make any decision for our future. The loss is greater for not making any decision versus making the wrong decision. By the way, one thing that we can do is to learn from our mistakes. Sometimes our failure creates a path for our success. Not all successful people make one attempt at success; it can take many tries and errors before making their way to the top. In those times of challenge, religion may come into play. People gather in the church for prayer and ask God for all kinds of help that they need to achieve their goals. In that moment of gathering, those who were discouraged and down find hope and mercy to revitalize their dream. In some churches, you feel so much love and joy it's not uncommon for people to lose hope during their challenging times, but who regain strength to work again on their dream. It's like an awakening.

The first Great Awakening can best be described as a revitalization of religious piety that swept through the American colonies between the 1730s and the 1770s. That revival was part of a much broader movement, an evangelical upsurge taking place simultaneously on the other side of the Atlantic, most notably in England, Scotland, and Germany. In all these Protestant cultures during the middle decades of the eighteenth century, a new Age of Faith rose to counter the currents of the Age of Enlightenment, to reaffirm the view that being truly religious meant trusting the heart rather than the head, prizing in feeling more than thinking, and relying on biblical revelation rather than human reason. One of the things that the bible teaches us and I see so many people put it into practice is faith. With faith, people overcome all kinds of life obstacles.

For the bible says, "And when he saw a fig tree in the way, he came to it, and found nothing thereon, but leaves only, and said unto it, Let no fruit grow on thee henceforward forever. And presently the fig tree withered away. And when the disciples saw it, they marvelled, saying, How soon is the fig tree withered away!" Jesus answered and said unto them, "Verily I say unto you, If ye have faith, and doubt not, ye shall not only do this which is done to the fig tree, but also if ye shall say unto this mountain, Be thou removed, and be thou cast into the sea; it shall be done." (Matthew 21:19-21) So we know that faith comes from God. It is the "gift of God." But He has given it to every believer. He has given to every believer the measure, or the same measure, of faith.

Notice also that God has done it (Rom. 12:3); it's not something that He is going to do. We're not trying to get faith. We're not praying for it. We have it. Every believer already has a measure of the God-kind of faith. You see, God gets everyone started off the same way. He doesn't give one person more faith than He gives another. He gives to every man the measure of faith. Then your faith grows according to what you do with it. A lot of people have done with their faith what the fellow in the Bible did with his one talent (see Matthew 25:25). They've just wrapped their faith up in a napkin, so to speak, and hidden it. They haven't used it at all. It's up to you what you do with the measure of faith God has given you. So the second thing I want you to know is this: This measure of faith can be increased. But you're the one who increases it, not God.

Certainly God furnishes the means whereby faith can be increased. But you increase your faith by doing two things: feeding it on the Word of God and exercising it—or putting it into practice. The Bible very often uses natural human terms to teach spiritual thoughts. For example, this is how Jesus taught in His earthly ministry, as we can read in the Gospels. We can conclude that faith can either be weak or strong. I am proving to you through Scripture that faith is measurable—that it can grow. We already mentioned that the Bible talks about growing faith (2 Thess. 1:3). Acts 6:5 says Stephen was full of faith. James 2:5 mentions rich faith. James 2:22 speaks of a perfect faith. First Timothy 1:5 speaks of unfeigned faith, or faith that is genuine and sincere. First Timothy 1:19 speaks of shipwrecked faith and of holding on to faith and to a good conscience. And First John 5:4 speaks of overcoming faith.

We know that the measure of faith given to every believer can grow. Your faith can be strengthened by feeding it on the Word of God and by exercising it or putting it into practice. F. Bosworth said, "Most Christians feed their body three hot meals a day and their spirit one cold snack a week. And they wonder why they're so weak in faith." Well, physically speaking, if you just ate one cold snack a week, you would grow weak physically! But the same is true spiritually. God's Word is faith food, and if we want our faith to grow, we must feed it more than once a week!

If you want your faith to grow, you have to start where you are. No one climbs a ladder starting on the top rung. You've got to start on the bottom rung and climb up if you're going to reach the top. That's the thing that defeats a lot of well-meaning Christians—they try to believe beyond their faith. Remember, just because someone has fed more on God's Word and has exercised his faith is not a sign that God has given him more faith than He gave someone else. No, the person who fed on the Word and exercised his faith had the same measure of faith to begin with as the others had. But he fed his faith and exercised it, and his faith grew strong! As a result he could believe God for more. So keep a positive attitude about your own faith. Recognize that you have faith and that you can cause it to grow. Feed your faith and exercise it right where you are in your Christian walk. Then your faith can grow and move mountains! Our faith is important in leading to inherit the promise of God because the Bible is so rich with God's promises, People faithfully believe and rely on them to sustain their life with no regard to seek earthly riches and continue living a moderate life often times full of joy.

When God told the Israelites to go in and possess the Promised Land, it appeared as though the Jordan River was an impenetrable barrier between them and the land of promise. You see, the river was at flood stage, and there was no way to cross it! God knew the Jordan River was there when He told the Israelites to cross over to their Promised Land. But still He gave the command to Joshua: .. . . "Arise, GO OVER THIS JORDAN, thou, and all this people, unto the land which I do give them." (Joshua 1:2).

How did God expect the Israelites to get across that river? Isn't it interesting that just because they ran into an impossibility, God didn't tell them they could quit. That impossible barrier didn't seem to bother God! It didn't make any difference to God that the Jordan River blocked the Israelites' passage into the Promised Land. Why? Because impossible barriers are nothing to God! Once again, God gave His people a plan so that by His strength and wisdom, they could accomplish the impossible. The Lord told Joshua to instruct the priests who were carrying the Ark of the Covenant to cross over the Jordan River first. The Lord said that as soon as the soles of their feet touched the water the Jordan River would stand up in a heap so all the people could pass over on dry ground. (Joshua 3:13).

In the natural, it sure didn't make any sense to send the priests into a river at flood stage. Flood-stage water is always swift water. That's why the news media today announces when there are flash-flood warnings. You're never supposed to get into fast-moving flood water because it will pull you under! Do you ever feel overwhelmed by the circumstances of life? Sometimes it seems as though adversity comes in like a flood and tries to sweep everything around you into its current—including you! And maybe, sometimes, you feel like you're hanging on for dear life.

When Joshua gave that command, you can understand why the priests might have thought, Joshua, the river is swift. We'll be swept away and drowned. But Joshua had heard from the Lord, and he'd seen the Lord's great faithfulness in all the miracles He had previously performed for the Israelites. Joshua was ready to obey God. If the people had just stood there without taking a step of faith, nothing would have happened. They had to be obedient to God's command and take that step of faith and get into the water! Faith takes action!

Has a river at flood stage come into your life, causing you a lot of problems? Instead of taking a step of faith, are you standing at the bank crying, :Lord, will You do something about the river?" God already told you to take up the Ark, so to speak, and cross the river. The Ark of the Covenant represents the Presence of God. When you're born again, you have the Presence of God living in you, and you have God's Word dwelling in your heart. If you'll just get up and take that first step of obedience, the Word dwelling in you will be a light to your feet, showing you exactly where to take the next step. And the Holy Spirit inside you will show you how to get across any river at flood stage in your life. But the Ark of God's Presence won't do you any good until you step out in faith and step into the water.

Faith and obedience bring God on the scene! God came through for those priests as soon as they stepped into the water. The Jordan parted so the rest of the Israelites could cross over on dry ground. You just need to take hold of God's Word and get in the water! Then you're going to see something happen in your life. You can stand on the sidelines all you want, waiting for God to do something, but the Lord is waiting for your obedience. The Lord promised that He would deliver you out of your problems, circumstances, and troubles, no matter what they may be. Whether your problems are spiritual, physical, financial, or something else, it makes no difference to the Lord! No matter how big the problem or flood seems to be, God will deliver you! Just standing on the edge of obedience with hope and wishful thinking won't get you across your river and into your promised land. It's time that you, as a believer, begin to speak the Word with authority over your situation. Then obediently move out in the power of the Holy Spirit to receive what belongs to you. Today is your day to begin possessing the promise! As believers, we are spiritually wealthy because of the exceedingly great promises we have in Jesus, our Savior.

"Do not be worried about your life, as to what you will eat or what you will drink; nor for your body, as to what you will put on. Is not life more than food, and the body more than clothing? Look at the birds of the air, that they do not sow, nor reap nor gather into barns, and yet your heavenly Father feeds them. Are you not worth much more than they? And who of you by being worried can add a single hour to his life? And why are you worried about clothing? Observe how the lilies of the field grow; they do not toil nor do they spin, yet I say to you that not even Solomon in all his glory clothed himself like one of these. But if God so clothes the grass of the field, which is alive today and tomorrow is thrown into the furnace, will He not much more clothe you? You of little faith! Do not worry then, saying, What will we eat?' or What will we drink?' or What will we wear for clothing?' For the Gentiles eagerly seek all these things; for your heavenly Father knows that you need all these things." (Matthew 6:25-32) "The Lord is the one who goes ahead of you; He will be with you. He will not fail you or forsake you. Do not fear or be dismayed." (Deuteronomy 31:8) "Do not fear, for I am with you; do not anxiously look about you, for I am your God. I will strengthen you, surely I will help you, surely I will uphold you with My righteous right hand." (Isaiah 41:10) "This is the confidence which we have before Him, that, if we ask anything according to His will, He hears us. And if we know that He hears us in whatever we ask, we know that we have the requests which we have asked from Him." (1 John 5:14-15) "The Lord God is a sun and shield; the Lord gives grace and glory; no good thing does He withhold from those who walk uprightly." (Psalm 84:11) "Blessed be the Lord, who daily bears our burden, the God who is our salvation." (Psalm 68:19) "Blessed be the God and

Father of our Lord Jesus Christ, the Father of mercies and God of all comfort, who comforts us in all our affliction so that we will be able to comfort those who are in any affliction with the comfort with which we ourselves are comforted by God." (2 Corinthians 1:3-4) "If any of you lacks wisdom, let him ask of God, who gives to all generously and without reproach, and it will be given to him." (James 1:5) "Come to Me, all who are weary and heavy-laden, and I will give you rest. Take My yoke upon you and learn from Me, for I am gentle and humble in heart, and you will find rest for your souls." (Matthew 11:28-29) "Be anxious for nothing, but in everything by prayer and supplication with thanksgiving let your requests be made known to God. And the peace of God, which surpasses all comprehension, will guard your hearts and your minds in Christ Jesus." (Philippians 4:6-7) "The righteous man will flourish like the palm tree, he will grow like a cedar in Lebanon. Planted in the house of the Lord, they will flourish in the courts of our God. They will still yield fruit in old age; they shall be full of sap and very green, to declare that the Lord is upright; He is my rock, and there is no unrighteousness in Him.." (Psalm 92:12-15) "God is our refuge and strength, a very present help in trouble. Therefore we will not fear, though the earth should change and though the mountains slip into the heart of the sea; though its waters roar and foam, though the mountains quake at its swelling pride." (Psalm 46:1-3)

Most believers are satisfied with being blessed by God—and mostly in the material realm alone. That is why Christian book stores are flooded with books on how one can be healed of one's sicknesses and become wealthy by tithing, etc. The emphasis is on physical and material wellbeing—health and prosperity. This is the clearest symptom of a self-centered life. And yet, we read in God's word, that Jesus died in order that we should no longer live for ourselves but only for Him (2 Cor. 5:15); in other words, not to please ourselves but only Him. Or to put it in yet another way, Jesus died in order to deliver us from a self-centered life, and to bring us into a God-centered life.

One of the things that can puzzle us these days is the way God blesses a lot of Christian work that is so thoroughly compromising in its character. Does this mean that God is not disturbed by the compromises and the deviations from His word? No, it certainly does not mean that God blesses many ministries that He cannot totally approve of.

Even when Moses disobeyed God's word and struck the rock (when God had told him to speak to it), God still 'blessed' that disobedient ministry. In fact, two million people were blessed through it. Yet God severely dealt with His disobedient servant afterwards (Num. 20:8-13). God blessed that ministry because He loved those two million needy people, not because He approved of what His servant did. It is even so today.

Many ministries are blessed because God loves the needy people who need salvation, healing, etc. But He certainly does not approve of much that goes on in the name of Jesus today. He will certainly punish the compromising preachers in due time.

The only condition to be fulfilled in order to get God's material blessings is that one must be either good or evil! For Jesus said that God sends sunshine and rain on both the righteous and the unrighteous (Matt. 5:45). Material blessing is therefore no sign of God's approval on one's life. Two million Israelites disobeyed God for forty years in the wilderness—so greatly that God was angry with them (Heb. 3:17). Yet God gave them food and healing throughout all those years—

and that too miraculously (Deut. 8:2). Even miraculous answers to prayer in the physical realm are therefore no indication that God is happy with a person's life.

God's approval, on the other hand, rested on Jesus when He was thirty years old, only because of one reason: Jesus had faithfully overcome temptation during all those years. He had lived a life centered in His Father and not in Himself. He never did what pleased Himself (Rom. 15:3). At His baptism, the Father testified, "This is My beloved Son, in whom I am well pleased" and not "This is My well-beloved Son whom I have blessed." The latter testimony would have meant nothing. It was the former, indicating God's approval, that meant everything for Jesus. To follow Jesus is to seek for the same testimony ourselves.

As children of Adam, we are all born self-centered. We grow up expecting everything to revolve around us and to serve us. When we get converted, we expect God also to serve us and bless us in various ways. We come to Him initially to be blessed with His forgiveness, and then go on to seek the blessings of healing, answers to prayer, material prosperity, employment, housing, marriage partner, etc. It is possible for our lives to be self-centered still, even when we are deeply 'religious' in our own and other people's eyes. God becomes just one more person in our 'orbit,' and we seek to get what we can out of Him.

The prodigal son came back in order to get food from his father; but the father still received him. God receives us even when our motives are utterly selfish. He loves us so much that He longs to receive us even when we come to Him with an obviously self-centered motive. His hope, however, is that we will mature quickly to realize that true spirituality is to partake of His own nature, which is to give, rather than to receive. With the vast majority of His children, however, God is never able to realize that purpose. They live and die in their self-centeredness thinking only of 'I', 'Me' and 'Mine' and of material and physical blessings.

To be mature is to have our mind renewed so that it is no longer centered on what we can get out of God, but rather on what God can get out of us in our one earthly life. This renewing of our mind is what brings transformation (Rom. 12:2). This is what qualified the 144,000 (in Rev. 14) to stand with the Lamb on Mount Zion.

True spirituality is not just getting victory over anger, irritability, lustful thoughts, love of money, etc. It is to cease living for oneself. It is to cease seeking our own—our own gain, our own comfort, our own convenience, our own will, our own rights, our own honour and even our own `spirituality.'

When the disciples asked Jesus to teach them to pray, He taught them a prayer that does not contain the words 'I', 'Me' or 'Mine' in it even once (Lk. 11:1-4). He taught us there to be concerned first about the Father's name, kingdom and will, and then to be concerned as much about our fellow believers (their material and spiritual welfare) as about ourselves ('us', 'us, 'us' and not 'me', 'me', 'me'). It is easy to learn that prayer 'by heart' and to repeat it like a parrot. But to learn that lesson in our heart requires that we truly forsake all and put God in the centre of our heart. The law that we will find most frequently in our members (Rom. 7:22), if we are honest in judging ourselves, will be the law of selfishness, the lust to seek our own convenience and our own rights all through life.

Jesus taught us to seek the kingdom of God first—that is to dethrone 'self' and to put God and His interests in the center of our life. Jesus gave up the comfort of heaven in order to do His Father's will on earth. Paul gave up the comfort of being a Christian businessman living luxuriously in Tarsus, in order to be an apostle, facing hardships for the Lord. Every one of the apostles lived that sacrificial God-centered life. They gave their all for the promotion of God's kingdom on earth, unlike many of today's 'tourist preachers'.

A holiness that still leaves us seeking our own comfort and convenience is a false holiness—even
if we have overcome anger and dirty thoughts. This is what many have not realized; and hence Satan has been able to deceive them. Many Christians travel or migrate to different countries seeking conveniences and comfort and wealth. They can still have God's blessings upon their lives, but not God's approval—for no one can serve both God and mammon (that is, wealth, pleasure, comfort, etc.). If we think that God's blessing on our lives and on our children is an indication that He is also happy with us, then Satan has truly deceived us. God's blessing and God's approval are two totally different things. At the end of our earthly lives, the testimony that we have should be the testimony that Enoch had before he left the earth: "He pleased God" (Heb. 11:5). Only three words—but no one can have a more powerful testimony to his earthly life. This is the testimony that Jesus and Paul had. To merely have a testimony that `He was blessed by God' is worth nothing, for millions of unbelievers, too, can have that testimony.

The beginnings of the First Great Awakening appeared among Presbyterians in Pennsylvania and New Jersey. Led by the Tennent family—Reverend William Tennent, a Scots-Irish immigrant, and his four sons, all clergymen—the Presbyterians not only initiated religious revivals in those colonies during the 1730s but also established a seminary to train clergymen whose fervid, heartfelt preaching would bring sinners to experience evangelical conversion. Originally known as "the Log College," it is better known today as Princeton University.

Religious enthusiasm quickly spread from the Presbyterians of the Middle Colonies to the Congregationalists (Puritans) and Baptists of New England. By the 1740s, the clergymen of these churches were conducting revivals throughout that region, using the same strategy that had contributed to the success of the Tennents. In emotionally-charged sermons, all the more powerful because they were delivered extemporaneously, preachers like Jonathan Edwards evoked vivid, terrifying images of the utter corruption of human nature and the terrors awaiting the unrepentant in hell. Hence Edwards's famous description of the sinner as a loathsome spider suspended by a slender thread over a pit of seething brimstone in his best known sermon, "Sinners in the Hands of an Angry God." The three most famed evangelical preachers of the Great Awakening, whose portraits do not convey the fiery emotions of their sermons. These early revivals in the northern colonies inspired some converts to become missionaries to the American South. In the late 1740s, Presbyterian preachers from New York and New Jersey began proselytizing in the Virginia Piedmont; and by the 1750s, some members of a group known as the Separate Baptists moved from New England to central North Carolina and quickly extended their influence to surrounding colonies. By the eve of the American Revolution, their evangelical converts accounted for about ten percent of all southern churchgoers.

The First Great Awakening also gained impetus from the wide-ranging American travels of an English preacher, George Whitefield. Although Whitefield had been ordained as a minister in the Church of England, he later allied with other Anglican clergymen who shared his evangelical bent, most notably John and Charles Wesley. Together they led a movement to reform the Church of England (much as the Puritans had attempted earlier to reform that church) which resulted in the founding of the Methodist Church late in the eighteenth century. During his several trips across the Atlantic after 1739, Whitefield preached everywhere in the American colonies, often drawing audiences so large that he was obliged to preach outdoors. What Whitefield preached was nothing more than what other Calvinists had been proclaiming for centuries—that sinful men and women were totally dependent for salvation on the mercy of a pure, all-powerful God. But Whitefield—and many American preachers who eagerly imitated his style—presented that message in novel ways. Gesturing dramatically, sometimes weeping openly or thundering out threats of hellfire-and-brimstone, they turned the sermon into a gripping theatrical performance.

But not all looked on with approval. Throughout the colonies, conservative and moderate clergymen questioned the emotionalism of evangelicals and charged that disorder and discord attended the revivals. They took great exception to "itinerants," ministers who, like Whitefield, traveled from one community to another, preaching and all too often criticizing the local clergy. And they took still greater exception when some white women and African Americans shed their subordinate social status long enough to exhort religious gatherings. Evangelical preachers and converts rejoined by lambasting their opponents as cold, uninspiring, and lacking in piety and grace. Battles raged within congregations and whole denominations over this challenge to clerical authority as well as the evangelical approach to conversion from "the heart. rather than 'the head'."

So the first Great Awakening left colonials sharply polarized along religious lines. Anglicans and Quakers gained new members among those who disapproved of the revival's excesses, while the Baptists (and, in the 1770s, the Methodists) made even more handsome gains from the ranks of radical evangelical converts. The largest single group of churchgoing Americans remained within the Congregationalist and Presbyterian denominations, but they divided internally between advocates and opponents of the Awakening, known respectively as "New Lights" and "Old Lights." Inevitably, civil governments were drawn into the fray. In colonies where one denomination received state support, other churches lobbied legislatures for disestablishment, an end to the favored status of Congregationalism in Connecticut and Massachusetts and of Anglicanism in the southern colonies.

Now let's cut to the classroom. You've sketched out the story of the first Great Awakening—its beginnings in the mid-Atlantic, its transit to New England, and its culmination in the South, its legacy of debate and division. And you've emphasized that it was only the colonial manifestation of a religious revival of much broader geographic scope—it spread the length of British North America (where, indeed, the only public figure whose name was known to virtually all colonials was George Whitefield!) and reverberated throughout the Protestant countries of Europe as well.

So your next move might be to pose the question: What could account for the tremendous appeal of evangelical Christianity to men and women living on both sides of the Atlantic during the latter half of the eighteenth century?

Chances are that most students will simply look confused at this inquiry—although some Christians among them might suggest that divine providence inspired large numbers of people to embrace "true Christianity." If that happens, you have a prime opportunity to point out that while such an explanation might well be persuasive from the standpoint of faith (that is, the perspective of a believer), historians (no matter what their personal religious convictions might be) strive to explain the IMMEDIATE causes of why things happened without reference to acts of God. (Otherwise they'd all be out of business, since the ULTIMATE cause of every historical event, from the standpoint of faith, is the will of God.)

With a little luck, those remarks will return the class to thinking about the SPECIFIC HISTORICAL CIRCUMSTANCES that might have enhanced the appeal of evangelical Christianity, with its formidable array of emotional consolations and moral certitudes, to large numbers of people in the eighteenth century.

To keep the discussion on that track—and to make such connections more accessible to students—you might try tossing out the observation that religious culture in America today bears many resemblances to that of the eighteenth century. As many commentators, both scholarly and popular, have noted, recent decades have witnessed an evangelical revival—what some regard as yet another "Great Awakening." Since the 1960s, membership in conservative evangelical Protestant churches has grown dramatically, while the membership of national organizations like the Promise Keepers and local bible study groups have also expanded at an astonishing rate. Some of your students will be aware of those trends—and therefore will have greater confidence when it comes to speculating about the social sources of contemporary evangelicalism's popular appeal—the transient lives of many Americans as population shifts to the South and West, the high incidence of family fragmentation in the face of staggering divorce rates, the uncertainty over gender roles fueled by feminism, the threats that recent scientific discoveries and "secular humanism" are perceived by many to pose to "traditional values," and so forth.

Okay, here's the payoff lurking at the end of this seeming digression into the religious culture of the late twentieth century: by now at least some students will see the connection between popular religious inclinations and broader social trends. So this is the moment for you to steer them back into the eighteenth century by noting that this, too, was an era of extraordinary upheaval and crisis for ordinary people. Remind them that England was entering the Industrial Revolution and that evangelicals like the Methodists attracted large numbers of converts among miners and factory workers. Remind them that northern Ireland and Germany, other hotbeds of evangelical enthusiasm, were wracked by warfare, famine, or both—harsh conditions that prompted hundreds of thousands to migrate to British North America. And, finally, remind them that in the American colonies, the same epoch witnessed a massive internal shift of population to the embattled frontiers of the South and West, where ordinary families endured hardscrabble, rootless lives and the ever-present threat of attack from dispossessed Indian tribes. Such circumstances also thrust women into newly responsible roles for the survival of migrating households as families were fragmented by movement and death.

Why would Jonathan Edwards refer to the Great Awakening as the "Surprising Work of God" in his 1737 narrative? It follows that men and women faced with such stark challenges might have sought opportunities for fellowship, solace, and emotional release—and that is exactly what evangelicals on both sides of the Atlantic offered. Presbyterians, Baptists, and Methodists touted their churches as havens from all the evils afflicting ordinary people—as islands of disciplined stability and Christian charity in a churning sea of social chaos and cultural confusion.

Chapter 4

Be Educated

Many of us believe that success is directly tied to education. When we talk about a good education, we talk a lot about success. We tend to take education itself as success in its own sphere. Does high education make one belong to the legit class? If it's the case, why do we have so many drop-out students? Why is everyone not forcing their way to high level education? I am not sure whether I should call it a mistake, but it happens that some people make the mistake by failing to go to school when they immigrate to America. They just come to seek only economic opportunity. In fact, they take School as a peripheral thing to do, or some of them believe that the education they acquired from their country is sufficient without any regard to some other things they need, such as speaking a new language that may *challenge* them by simply living in this country. Even if you have been highly educated in your country, integration into a new country, new culture sometimes requires reformation. Communication can be the number one challenge that you may have to face.

Language is more than just a means of communication. It influences our culture and even our thought processes. During the first four decades of the 20th century, language was viewed by American linguists and anthropologists as being more important than it actually is in shaping our perception of reality. This was mostly due to Edward Sapir and his student Benjamin Whorf who said that language predetermines what we see in the world around us. In other words, language acts like a polarizing lens on a camera in filtering reality—we see the real world only in the categories of our language.

Cross cultural comparisons of such things as color terms were used by Sapir and Whorf as evidence of this hypothesis. When we perceive color with our eyes, we are sensing that portion of electromagnetic radiation that is visible light. In fact, the spectrum of visible light is a continuum of light waves with frequencies that increase at a continuous rate from one end to the other. In other words, there are no distinct colors like red and green in nature. Our culture, through language, guides us in seeing the spectrum in terms of the arbitrarily established categories that we call colors. Different cultures may divide up the spectrum in different ways. This can be seen in the comparison of some English language colors with their counterparts in the Tiv language of Nigeria:

Sapir and Whorf interpreted these data as indicating that colors are not objective, naturally determined segments of reality. In other words, the colors we see are predetermined by what our culture prepares us to see. This example used to support the Sapir-Whorf hypothesis that was objectively tested in the 1960's. That research indicated that they went too far. All normal humans share similar sense perceptions of color despite differences in color terminology from one language to another. The physiology of our eyes is essentially the same. People all over the world can see subtle gradations of color and can comprehend other ways of dividing up the spectrum of visible light. However, as a society's economy and technology increase in complexity, the number of color terms usually also increases. That is to say, the spectrum of visible light gets subdivided into more categories. As the environment changes, culture and language typically respond by creating new terminology to describe it.

The U.S. Census Bureau estimates that more than 300 languages are spoken in the United States. The bureau divides those languages into four categories: Spanish; other Indo-European languages, which includes German, Yiddish, Swedish, French, Italian, Russian, Polish, Hindi, Punjabi, Greek and several others; Asian and Pacific Island languages, including Chinese, Korean, Japanese, Thai, Tamil and more; and "all other languages," which is a category for languages that didn't fit into the first three categories, such as Hungarian, Arabic, Hebrew, languages of Africa and languages of native people of North, Central and South America

There is no official language of the United States, according to the U.S. government. While almost every language in the world is spoken in the United States, Spanish, Chinese, French and German are among the most frequently spoken non-English languages. Ninety percent of the U.S. population speaks and understands at least some English, and most official business is conducted in English. Therefore, speaking a good English language is important (not necessary) for your venture as an immigrant and crucial for your development plan. The way to achieve a good articulated language is through the means of education—going to school.

In our eyes, education is everything, but there are other ingredients that are equally or even more important on the path to success. Higher education is particularly crucial for anyone wanting to enter a specialty field; like becoming an accountant, financial adviser, lawyer or doctor. But there are many other careers that, especially when embraced with vigor, can be mastered through self-determination, experience, and self-education.

Education is the process of learning and knowing, which is not restricted to our school text-books. It is a complete process and unbroken through our life. Even the regular happenings and events around us educate us, in one or the other way. It would not be an exaggeration to say that the existence of human beings is fruitless without education. An educated person has the ability to change the world, as he/she is brimming with confidence and assured of making the right moves. The education dwells on the importance of everyone's lives.

Education makes a worthy contribution to our lives, by making us responsible citizens. We get to know our history and culture through education and absorb those values. Education opens our mind and expands our horizon. It enables us to understand our duties as a citizen and encourages us to follow them. There is no denying the fact that an educated person is a better citizen.

Education is futuristic in character, in so far that it ensures that the one who receives good education gets a secure future. Our productivity is increased by acquiring new skills and talents through education. We find ourselves in the most competitive jobs, courtesy of the right training and education. The importance of education is evident by the wobbly heights we achieve in life.

Education can open a new life for us. The significance of education, to a great part, lies in its ability to open new life for us. It expands our outlook and teaches us to be tolerant towards other views. An educated person will find it easier to understand a different point of view than the one who is uneducated. Education broadens our mental landscape and is the way forward to greater enlightenment—the ultimate goal of every human in life.

Education Spreads our Awareness. Awareness is a virtue in itself, given that the lack of awareness is lamented everywhere. Education spreads awareness, informing us about our rights and the services that we can access. On the most basic notes, it teaches us to differentiate between right and wrong. For most parts of our lives, we falter in dichotomizing right and wrong, but the right education gives us the right answers.

Education Helps In Decision-Making. Decision making is an integral part of our life. We have to take decisions throughout our lives and sometimes, decision making can be a very tough and challenging process. It can leave us perplexed and often wondering, as to what is the right choice. Education is significant, because it enables us to take the right decisions and prevents losses.

An educated person is a confident person. Education fosters a positive outlook and allows us to believe in ourselves. Self-belief is the most wanted trait in a human being and education leads us toward relying on ourselves, making us believe that we are ready to take on the world.

At the end of the day, it is learning, and not necessarily 'formal education,' that is your ticket to success. Learning is your own responsibility—at every stage of your life. Your self-education can be the most significant single factor (that you have complete control over) that can have the greatest impact on your personal success. Most people who are successful have some sort of formal education. Education makes you able to set, organize, manage and control your path to success. On the contrary, a lack of education can put you on a rocky road to drive to your destiny. What do I mean by that? It means a place that could take an hour's drive to your destination ends up taking you double time or even more time to pass the entire milestone. As a result, the amount
of time you could spend to enjoy the fruit of your work is being wasted in the struggle with an unpaved road.

There is a great deal of discussion today about the importance of a college degree. According to the U.S. Department of Labor, 90 percent of the fastest-growing jobs in the future will require some postsecondary education or training. If you look at who has fared best in this economic downturn, there is a direct correlation between the unemployment rate and one's level of educational attainment.

Yet we also hear we are falling short. Not long ago, the United States used to have the highest number of college graduates among industrialized nations. Currently, we are in 13th place. This has significant ramifications on our strength as a nation, as well as our ability to compete in the global economy.

After decades of failed education policies, scientists, economists and educators are beginning to rethink their basic ideas about what it takes to succeed in school. They're beginning to look at so-called "non-cognitive skills" — grit, perseverance, conscientiousness, and optimism; for instance — and wondering if they might be as important as cognitive skills.

The idea comes at a key time for U.S. education. A decade after Congress passed the No Child

Left Behind law, educators are as divided as ever on the law's key goal: how to improve educational outcomes for poor children. On one side, an influential group of educators say the stresses and deprivations of poverty doom kids' aspirations—cure poverty, they say, and education will follow. On the other side are educators who say a more competitive, focused and accountable education system will lift kids out of poverty by giving them a ticket to college and the middle class.

But, so far, we haven't cured poverty, and the results from several "no excuses" experiments are mixed. Alumni of the highly regarded KIPP middle schools for low-income students, for instance, boast excellent high school graduation rates. But few make it through college.

New research suggests that a third way might be more practical: Alleviate the effects of poverty by helping parents raise more resilient kids — and helping kids develop habits of mind to persevere through difficulty.

"We haven't been able to solve big problems because we've been looking in the wrong places," writes author Paul Tough, whose new book, *How Children Succeed*, is reigniting interest in the topic. Among those heeding the new research: David Levin, a KIPP co-founder who adopted a 24-item "character report card" in the face of poor college-going results. After more than a decade of no-nonsense academics and harsh discipline, "He (Levin) had created the perfect middle-school student, but he hadn't created the perfect college student," said Tough. KIPP students now sit for parent-teacher conferences that detail not just how they're doing in history and algebra, but how well they score on zest, curiosity, social intelligence, and optimism.

"When we think about the word 'character,' we often think of something that is not at all changeable — it's just like what you're born with," Tough says. "But these strengths are things that are absolutely changeable. Individuals can change them themselves. Teachers and parents can have a huge impact on how they're developed."

A former editor of the New York Times Magazine, Tough says the need to develop grit doesn't just occupy educators of low-income kids. He writes that many elite schools offer students not so much a chance to succeed as "a high probability of nonfailure" — and connections that ensure a student never falls out of the upper class.

Indeed, says Dominic Randolph, headmaster of Riverdale Country School in the Bronx, "In most highly academic environments in the United States, no one fails anything."

Tough also details the efforts of Elizabeth Spiegel, a chess teacher at a Brooklyn middle school who develops master players. She does it, Tough discovers, by painstakingly teaching her students to reflect on every move of every game — mistakes included. Her players write out each move and review them afterward, drilling down to figure out why they made a mistake and how to fix it. "Teaching chess is really about teaching the habits that go along with thinking," Spiegel tells him.

She likens the process to psychotherapy, saying her players often make the same mistakes repeatedly. In the end, she says, they must find a way to separate themselves from their mistakes and losses. "I try to teach my students that losing is something you do, not something you are," she says.

The results speak for themselves: Spiegel's teams and individual players both consistently rank among the best nationwide, and a few students achieve grand master status before they turn 13. After one young player, James Black, beats Ukranian-born international chess master Yuri Lapshun, the defeated Ukranian sits down with James and Spiegel to analyze the game. Move by move, the teacher realizes, James has totally outplayed one of the best players in the world. In the end, she tells James he'd played "exceptionally deep chess."

Are there any academic and social supports available to students to help them along the way? Are there peer mentors? Faculty mentors? Is there a bridge program, summer immersion, or orientation program that can help the student make the transition to college successfully? In the work at the National College Advising Corps, we call these "best match" and "best fit" questions.

The concept of "college match," as defined by the Consortium on Chicago School Research at the University of Chicago in their 2008 report titled "From High School to the Future: Potholes on the Road to College," documents that a student who applies to and enrolls in a college or university with an admission selectivity rating that matches his/her academic qualifications is more likely to succeed in school and attain a college degree.

The report showed that the academic match of students based on their unweighted GPAs and their most recent ACT/SAT score to the selectivity rating of the post-secondary institution they enrolled in was a critical key to completion rates and success.

The research concluded with the shocking finding that "across all students, two-thirds (62 percent) of students attended a college with a selectivity level that was below the kinds of colleges they would have most likely been accepted to given their level of academic qualifications."

This concept is called "under-matching" and has been further documented by William Bowen, Matthew Chingos, and Michael McPherson in their book, *Crossing the Finish Line*. Students need to attend schools that they are ready for academically. And likewise, they need to attend schools that are prepared to offer them the courses and support that will get them to the finish line.

Academic match is not the end of the story, however. Several colleges may be a good match academically for a student, but which college is the best "fit"?

The same 2008 report found that students are more likely to persist in college and graduate successfully if, in addition to academic match, they have also considered other factors to determine overall fit. These factors include: financial viability, majors and programs offered, support services, social/emotional fit, and the college's persistence and graduation rates.

As we begin another academic year, let's help our students find the right match and fit. Let's find them schools that will serve them well. Whether it is a credential, vocational school, community college, or university, it is about honoring the investment and honoring our future. It's about success.

During their high school career, students may begin to question the importance of a college education. They might find themselves asking: "Why is it important to go to college?" The answer is that, more than ever, attending college provides opportunities for graduates which are not as widespread to those who have not received a higher education.

For many high school students, being able to immediately generate an income after graduation is an appealing thought. They may also be repelled by the rising cost of tuition, and while it is true that a higher education may be one of the largest expenses you will ever face, the importance of a college education has become quite evident in terms of earning potential within today's economy

One important answer to this question is more opportunity. As opposed to generations of the past, high school graduates today are unable to obtain the number of high-paying jobs that were once available. The U.S. has been transformed from a manufacturing-based economy to an economy based on knowledge; the importance of a college education today can be compared to that of a high school education forty years ago. It serves as the gateway to better options and more opportunity.

There are additional reasons as to why it is important to go to college. When students experience a post secondary education, they have the opportunity to read books and listen to the lectures of top experts in their fields. This stimulation encourages students to think, ask questions, and explore new ideas, which allows for additional growth and development and provides college graduates with an edge in the job market over those who have not experienced a higher education.

The importance of a college education is also accentuated because of the opportunity to gain valuable resources during their tenure. The more connections which are collected during your college career, the more options you will have when you begin your job search. Once you have ended your job search and have started your career, however, the importance of a college education has not been exhausted. Having a college degree often provides for greater promotion opportunity.

So, why should you go to college? The reasoning does not begin and end with the job aspect. A good education is beneficial from many different viewpoints, and while the importance of a college education is quite evident for many high school students, what is often not as clear is how they will pay for that education.

Although the colleges and universities of today carry a heavy price tag, it is of great importance not to let that discourage you from obtaining a college education. While the cost of tuition continues to rise, so too does the number of available financial aid options. Below we will explain why it is important to explore these options before you go to college and the large payoff they often provide.

From local and federal options, to categorical and corporate options, college-bound students have a variety of opportunities worth exploring when attempting to obtain financial aid. A common misrepresentation of financial aid packages (e.g. scholarships, grants, loans, work study programs) is that they provide funding for an entire college education. The reality is that most of these packages are smaller and it may take several of them to add up. This is why it is important to explore all of your options before you go to college:

Local options

The people of your own community fully understand the importance of a college education, which is why organizations such as the American Legion, the Rotary Club, the Jaycees, and Boosters chapters offer scholarships for high school students in the area. These organizations are often overlooked and serve as a great resource due to the fact that they have far less competition than national awards. Start your local search by visiting your high school's career options to see what is available.

Federal options

The federal government is also well aware of the importance of a college education, which is why they award more financial aid to college-bound students than any other resource. The most important step in obtaining federal aid is to fill out the Free Application for Federal Student Aid (FAFSA). Follow this link for more information on filing the FAFSA for financial aid.

Merit-based options

Merit scholarships are awarded to students based on academic or athletic abilities, as well as categories such as ethnicity, religious affiliation, club membership, interests, talent or career plans. Learn more about merit-based options by following this link: College Scholarship Money

Corporate options

Corporations are another resource which understands the vast importance of a college education. Every year, corporations ranging from Target to Coca-Cola offer financial aid to thousands of college-bound students. A great way to start your corporate scholarship search is with you or your spouse's company. Often times, organizations will award the children of employees with scholarships or grants. Follow this link to learn more about college financial aid and grant searches and determine the eligibility of your student.

Understanding the Importance of College Education

If you are still asking yourself why should you go to college, it is important to remember the significant amount of opportunity available for college graduates. The global economy is becoming increasingly more competitive, and in order to give yourself the best chance for a well-paying job, you must first understand the importance of college education.

Attending college provides students with the knowledge and experience they are unable to receive from a secondary education, and finding a way to fund a higher education now can pay off in a huge way in the years to come.

The educational aspirations Americans hold for their children have never been higher than they are today. The demand for education is contagious and readily transferred from generation to generation. Parents want more and better schooling for their children than they had ever had. The need for unskilled and uneducated labor has almost vanished, and the need for highly educated labor continues to be in great demand. However education has its expenses and not everyone is able to financially afford to be better educated. The federal government has put its best foot forward to help with citizens who need extra money for their education. Thanks to the G.I. Bill, National Defense Education Act (NDEA), and the Elementary and Secondary Education Act (ESEA) many Americans have been able to reach higher education.

The "G.I. Bill of Rights" is a body of federal legislation which has provided educational and other benefits for veterans of World War II. Over 11 million persons have availed themselves of these benefits. A general aim for this legislation has been to compensate veterans for their sacrifices and services. Another important reason, however, has been the necessity (particularly in the 1940's) of reintegrating the numbers of returning servicemen into the civilian economy and into national life. No review could possibly describe the massive impact of the World War II G.I. Bill on the nation or the individual lives of veterans who were aided through this program and have since graduated with careers as doctors, lawyers, engineers, teachers, accountants, mechanics, clergymen, and farmers. Many historians have rated the G.I. Bill of Rights one of the most enlightened pieces of legislation ever enacted by the Congress of the United States. Some describe it as one of the most successful experiments in socioeconomic expansion undertaken by the U.S. government. Certainly, as long as U.S. citizens continue to be drafted for military service, this kind of legislation will remain high on the legislative priority list.

In 1958 Congress passed the National Defense Education Act (NDEA) which appropriated federal funds to improve instruction in those areas considered crucial to national defense and security. The areas that were considered were mathematics, foreign languages, and science. Between 1945 and 1958, there was intense debate about federal aid to elementary and secondary schools. Special interests and political dynamics blocked the enactment of federal aid legislation.

However, in 1957 the political situation changed when the Soviet Union, the rival of the United States in the Cold War successfully orbited Sputnik, a space satellite. The Soviet space success and well-publicized American space failures created a climate of national crisis. Critics pointed to the deficiencies of American students in mathematics and science. The Sputnik crisis sparked national legislation to support training, equipment, and programs in fields vital to defense. The scientific community including university scholars and curriculum specialists are often called upon to reconstruct subject-matter content, especially on the high school level.

Another program that increased federal financial involvement still further was the Elementary and Secondary Education Act (ESEA) of 1965. Whereas the NDEA emphasized science and mathematics, the ESEA was a federal response to the significant social change taking place in American society. Many African American students as well as members of other minority groups, especially in inner- city areas, were educationally disadvantaged because of social and economic conditions. The ESEA related to President Lyndon Johnson's program,"War on Poverty," which encouraged special programs for children of low-income families. It also created a range of early childhood educational programs for economically and culturally disadvantaged children. These programs had an impact on early childhood education not only for minority children but for all children. When the ESEA was passed it immediately provided $1-billion to supplement and improve the education of economically disadvantaged children. In 1981, Title I of ESEA was revised and is now named Chapter 1 of the Educational Consolidation and Improvement Act (ECIA). In 1992 Chapter 1 funding was nearly $7 billion. Research indicates that Chapter 1 programs still do not ensure students will acquire the academic and intellectual skills necessary for obtaining good jobs in a modern economy, however, Chapter 1 students typically gain a year in reading and math achievement for each year of participation in elementary grades, and thus no longer fall further behind their advantaged peers. Various problems do persist and many disadvantaged students receive only one or two years of compensatory services and then tend to decline in relative achievement. Participants who start out far behind national achievement averages usually remain there, and many of the Chapter 1 programs conducted nationally are poorly implemented and ineffective.

This chapter emphasizes the importance of education that has been embraced by the greatest country on earth— the United States of America. If the United States of America stresses the importance of education to help you compete in global economics, how much more do immigrants to this country need to accentuate education in order to integrate themselves into this fast-paced competitive country.

The next chapter will take you inside the labor work force from the life of those who don't have a high level of education to obtain a high-paying job versus those who are highly educated.

Chapter 5

American working Life

It is commonly known that many countries around the world don't offer the same work opportunities for all classes of citizens, which is why so many people leave their countries to join the work force in America. Although a great percentage of them are coming for many different reasons, their arrival and their desire to join the work force oftentimes is for survival. By doing so without any skill set, more than 90 % of them quickly fall into the category of low income people before they can meet the requirement necessary to obtain higher income jobs. Of course, some people know how to swim faster than others to get out of that low income river. Some view it as a normal life as it is better than back home because it may be the first time that they ever have a check in their entire life, while others look at it as a transitional path for a better life. No matter how one looks at it, it's the first taste of freedom—Freedom to work. For this reason, many people experience some great joy in that moment. The fact that they become financially independent, they enjoy tremendous power: power to buy, power to decide, power to help others and you name it. While going through the transitional period is kind of tricky; one mistake we should avoid making as an immigrant is spending every penny you make. We need to save as much as we can from the beginning; no matter what road you take later on, you are going to need financial support. Financial support is very important, especially for those who dream big and want to achieve big. This country is not like the third world countries where you can start a business with $10 or turn a very small amount of money quickily and easily into a big trunk of cash. The capitalist system requires more than that. There may be a minimal number of people who started with almost nothing and luckily, in the blink of an eye, make their way to horizon, but that chance is uncertain.

One of the things that may help you a lot as a foreigner who immigrates to America who has great plan for success is to avoid premature relationships. Having a family is great, but to rush into a relationship that you are not ready for has serious consequences. Despite everything appearing new and beautiful should not be an occasion for you to forget your dream. Jumping quickly into a relationship may ruin your life altogether. All that glitters is not gold. Living a single life can be boring, but having a bad relationship is ironically detriment to someone's life. The impact can be a stumbling block for your development in life. When you fall the first time, you may not be able to rise again. Not everyone who falls has a chance to get back on their feet. Or, once you fall the first time, you are at a very high risk to fall again. Life is not stagnant, one has to progress or backslide. In that condition, backsliding will be the expected choice. I see so many folks who got trapped in a bad relationship, even though they describe it as painful, they cannot stop it. Thus they start jumping from one relationship to another. By so doing, the chance to contract a sexually transmitted disease is at very high risk.

Disease has a great impact on society, both as an illness and as a source of discrimination. The disease also has significant economic impacts. There are many misconceptions about disease such as HIV/AIDS that many people believe can be transmitted by casual non-sexual contact. The disease has also become the subject of many controversies involving religion. It has attracted international medical and political attention as well as large-scale funding since it was identified in the 1980s. Your dream may be shattered by the news of contracting such an illness.

Avoiding a dreadful pain is the key to living a healthy life to walk toward your goal. Although there are plenty of people who are affected by this disease, the work force needs to say that their productivity cannot be the same as that of healthy persons. When they face challenges that involve the work place, such as stress, pressures and humiliations, they may become too flaky (unreliable) to sustain those forces.

Let's see what is involved in the work force in America.

You may have heard that life here is very easy compared to that in other countries. In some ways it is east, since Americans enjoy a high standard of living, but many Americans work long hours. Life here can be very fast paced in comparison to some other cultures. The work ethic is very strong in this country, and the business arena can be a competitive one where productivity is expected. A typical business here opens its doors around 9 a.m. (this can vary some), with a short break for lunch at noontime (1/2 hour) and then stays open until 5:30. A typical workday means 8 hours of working, with the noon break, and occasionally a ten minute break during the mid-morning or afternoon. Some businesses have longer hours, and expect employees to put in overtime routinely. The pace at businesses will vary. Some businesses are high pressured and competitive, and the pace is busy all day long; others may be more relaxed, but expectations are usually high no matter the pace. Being late or calling in sick too often is frowned on, and while most businesses will have a certain number of sick days allotted for the year they encourage workers to not use them unless really necessary. The good news is that most businesses will have good benefits such as vacation days, medical and dental insurance, and other options; and employees who work hard are often given promotions or raises as time goes on.

The Economic Policy Institute reports that approximately 24 percent (almost one-fourth) of all American workers today earn below-poverty incomes ($8.71 an hour or less.) Low-income workers tend to be women and people of color, and their low incomes often result from low hourly wages at contingent, short hours, or temporary jobs (usually without benefits.) For low-paid workers, long work hours—if they can get them—are often essential

Recent studies have painted a grim picture of the American working world: Longer days, less vacation time, later retirement, and — that was all during the good years of the 1990s.
The last few months have done nothing to ease those conditions, adding job insecurity to the mix as an increasing number of companies lay off workers to "downsize" in the slumping economy. Those lucky enough to still have a job can expect to be asked to do more, to make up for the "streamlined" workforce. Not only are Americans working longer hours than at any time since statistics have been kept, but now they are also working longer than anyone else in the industrialized world. And while workers in other countries have been seeing their hours cut back by legislation focused on preventing work from infringing on private life, Americans have been going in the other direction.

Some books have been embraced by a public that apparently feels harassed by the pressures of the workplace. Road rage, workplace shootings, the rising number of children placed in day care and the increasing demand on schools to provide after-school activities to occupy children whose parents are too busy have all been pointed to as evidence that Americans are overstressed and overworked. The Bureau of Labor statistics released last year confirmation of what Fraser had been hearing in four years of interviews with white-collar workers. In 1999, more than 25 million Americans— 20.5 percent of the total workforce—reported that they worked at least 49 hours a week, and 11 million of those said they worked more than 59 hours a week.

We find out that about one in four workers, age 18 to 61, earned less than $7.73 an hour in 2003. Low-wage workers who reside in low-income families with children are substantially less educated than the average worker, are concentrated in industries with low wages, and have limited prospects for wage growth. Many policies aimed at low-wage workers are not well-targeted to workers in low-income families with children, in part because only one in four low-wage workers reside in such families. Nevertheless, policies targeted at low-wage workers may have broad benefits, including improving the lot of low-income families with children.

The phrase ."low-wage workforce" conjures an image of men and women struggling to support their families, toiling away at menial jobs for bosses who consider them expendable. To address the problem of "low-wage jobs," advocates have called for the public sector to expand work-support programs, such as earned income tax credits, wage subsidies, training programs, and to impose mandates to raise worker pay through minimum wage increases, provide benefits like health insurance and paid time off, and protection of jobs. In addition, some private-sector employers have implemented practices offering workers more flexibility in scheduling and time off because these employers find that these practices improve productivity and reduce the costs associated with high staff turnover.

This provides a solid empirical foundation for these discussions by defining and documenting the characteristics of low-wage workers and their employers. In particular, we focus on low-wage workers who reside in low-income families and support children. We use nationally representative data from the 2004 Annual Demographic Supplement to the Current Population Survey for our analysis.

We find that low-wage workers who reside in low-income families with children are substantially less educated and are concentrated in industries with low wages and poor prospects for wage growth. Many policies targeted at low-wage workers are not well targeted at workers in low-income families with children, in part, because they are a small subset of the low-wage workforce. Nevertheless, policies targeted at low-wage workers may have broad benefits, including improving the lot of low-income families with children. Further, other policies, such as child care policies, can address the needs of low-income families with children, and some policies, such as improving career-focused education, may have long-term benefits at relatively low cost. To pay for mandated benefits, employers may reduce their workers' wage rates, restrict wage growth, or simply use less labor. Alternatively, they may accept smaller profit margins, reduce the compensation of more highly paid workers, or pass the costs on to consumers in the form of higher prices. Employers become smart by cutting off worker compensation benefits, employees are then forced to look for help in the disability benefit system that is, presumably, available for disabled people.

Those who argue that the disability system has become choked with exaggerated claims are not entirely wrong. In 2011, the Wall Street Journal reported on David Daugherty, a West Virginia judge who had seemingly rubber-stamped approval for all but four of the 1,284 disability appeals that came before him. He appeared to be colluding with a lawyer named Eric Conn, who had advertised his services on billboards as "Mr. Social Security" and sometimes brought "an inflatable replica of himself to events." It's faster for disability judges to approve a disability claim than to reject one, so it's easy to see how less-than-deserving cases would sneak through.

Because of rising income inequality, poor people can now earn almost as much on disability as they can at minimum-wage jobs—as long as they can prove they're sick enough. In a 2006 analysis, the economists David Autor and Mark Duggan found that the main reason disability rolls have swollen is that the program's rules were liberalized in 1984. The Social Security administration was directed to weigh applicants' pain and discomfort more heavily and to relax its mental illness screening. (The government has four different sets of standards: one for people under the age of 50, another for those between 50 and 54, another for 55-59-year-olds, and a final one for those 60 and older.)

To sign up, applicants first state their disabilities and the names of their doctors. Each application is reviewed by state officials and sometimes by an independent doctor. Two-thirds of applicants are rejected after this step because they lack medical documentation that their ailments will keep them out of work for at least a year. From there, an applicant can appeal, and a different official will review his or her paperwork. After that, another 11 percent of applications are approved.

The rejected cases are seen by administrative judges in courtrooms across the country. According to a recent Washington Post investigation, the entire process can take years. If they make it through, beneficiaries will receive $13,740 annually, on average.

The problem is, even if society were to decide that there should be fewer people on disability, the system has become too bloated with sneaky pretenders, and it isn't clear what a fifth of the population of Grundy would do to survive. It's entirely possible that some of the town's residents are faking their disability claims, but it's hard to imagine that most of them are. People who are rolling in undeserved government dough generally don't line up at the crack of dawn to get their teeth fixed in an elementary school cafeteria.

Residents of Grundy sometimes run into problems during their legal proceedings, which take place via video chat from a courthouse over the mountains in Bluefield. The judge, who is listening to the arguments remotely, must consider age, education, and whether the applicant's skills can be transferred to another line of work."If you are physically or mentally able to do a job, you don't meet the test for disability," Wegbreit says. "It doesn't matter if that job does or doesn't exist in your region of the country. And that job doesn't exist in Buchanan county."

Enough applications get through that disability benefits provide an economic safety net to Buchanan county residents. But the high number of recipients also depresses the area further by keeping new businesses away. Companies aren't eager to hire sick, worn-out miners.

"This area is a nightmare of disability," Smiddy says. Any company starting a business here knows that a substantial percentage of workers ."are going to have dust on their lungs, they're going to be obese, they've already smoked a pack a day."

Because of rising income inequality, poor people can now earn as much on disability as they can at minimum-wage jobs—as long as they can prove they're sick enough.

Once people get on disability, they usually don't go back to gainful employment. Though they're not counted in unemployment statistics, functionally, they become like the long-term unemployed—falling into an economic hole from which it is notoriously hard to claw out.

Employed people might think of being out of work as being relaxing, but jobs provide identity and purpose. "Whatever the job, it can give a sense of belonging, of being a contributor; an important part, however menial, of an organization with a bigger purpose, a valued part of society," wrote Tom Fryers, a visiting professor of public health at the University of Leicester in the U.K., in a recent paper. "Work can provide a structure for the day, week, and year without which life just drifts by."

Idleness, meanwhile, further depletes bodies and minds. The rate of depression is 19 percent among people who have been unemployed for a year, compared to just 10 to 11 percent for people who went without jobs for just a few weeks. Even though they don't face the same financial strains as the long-term unemployed, people on disability still suffer the negative health effects of being jobless. Researchers have also found high rates of depression among recipients on welfare, for example.

"Once you're on the couch, your muscles become weak, you're going to gain weight, you're not physically capable of going back in the coal mine," Smiddy said. A lack of work has been shown to increase the risk of premature death significantly, particularly for men.

The problem, as Smiddy sees it, it isn't just that the economy is limited, or that the region's education and medical systems could use an overhaul. The county's health has been so poor for so long, he says, that locals have set their expectations too low. And once everyone—the people, their employers, their doctors, the government—accepts that bleak vision, it hardens into reality. It makes it so there's no life after coal.

.It's 'Just pull my teeth', or 'Grandpa died when he was 50' or 'Momma's already on oxygen,'. Smiddy tells me, his voice growing increasingly exasperated as he clicks through x-rays in his makeshift office. "There's a negative fatalistic attitude. We have to have an expectation of health, and seek health."

Indications are that the bulk of those overworked people were white collar workers, who do not punch a clock and whose hours therefore are the most difficult to track.

Schor's 1997 book, which became a bestseller, stated that in 1990 Americans worked an average of nearly one month more per year than they had in 1970. Statistics indicate that the trend she described hasn't been reversed in the last decade.

Ciulla's book is perhaps a less pessimistic — and broader — look at Americans' relationship to the workplace, but she shares Schor's view that, more than ever before, work dominates people's lives in this country.

Not everyone has agreed with the conclusions the three authors drew from studying the various statistical surveys of Americans at work, from Fortune magazine polls for Fortune 500 CEOs, to International Labor Organization studies of workers around the world, and from talking to American workers themselves.

The dissenters point to evidence that workers consistently overestimate the amount of time they spend on the job, and thus discount studies based on information from workers themselves. Instead, they look at surveys based on worker hours as reported by employers, though that leaves overtime hours worked by salaried employees unaccounted for.

The other evidence often pointed to that people are not really working as much as they say is the increasing number of part-time jobs. How can people be working more if more people are not working full-time?

But the anecdotal evidence presented by Fraser, Schor and Ciulla—and met by millions of people everyday—is that Americans feel they are working more than ever.

Update, 3/6/2013: The Dow hit a record high on Tuesday, but who's winning? The conditions of America's jobless recovery detailed in this writing nearly two years ago have only continued—corporate earnings have risen at an annualized rate of 20 percent since the end of 2008, according to the New York Times, while Americans' disposable income has inched ahead 1.4 percent by comparison. Or, as a top economist for Bank of America told the Times, "So far in this recovery, corporations have captured an unusually high share of the income gains." Here's why.

On a bright spring day in a wisteria-bedecked courtyard full of earnest, if half-drunk, conference attendees, we were commiserating with a fellow journalist about all the jobs we knew of that were going unfilled, being absorbed or handled "on the side." It was tough for all concerned, but necessary—you know, doing more with less.

His old-school phrase gave form to something we'd been noticing with increasing apprehension—and it extended far beyond journalism. We'd hear from creative professionals in what seemed to be dream jobs who were crumbling under ever-expanding to-do lists; from bus drivers, hospital technicians, construction workers, doctors, and lawyers who shame-facedly whispered that no matter how hard they tried to keep up with the extra hours and extra tasks, they just couldn't hold it together. Also read harrowing first-person tales of overwork and 12 charts on just how much is being demanded of American workers.

Webster's defines speedup as "an employer's demand for accelerated output without increased pay," and it used to be a household word. Bosses would speed up the line to fill a big order, to goose profits, or to punish a restive workforce. Workers recognized it, unions (remember those?) watched for and negotiated over it—and, if necessary, walked out over it.

But now we no longer even acknowledge it—not in blue-collar work, not in white-collar or pink-collar work, not in economics texts, and certainly not in the media (except when journalists gripe about the staff-compacted-job-expanded newsroom). Now the word we use is "productivity," a term insidious in both its usage and creep. The not-so-subtle implication is always: Don't you want to be a productive member of society? Pundits across the political spectrum revel in the fact that U.S. productivity (a.k.a. economic output per hour worked) consistently leads the world. Yes, year after year, Americans wring even more value out of each minute on the job than we did the year before. U-S-A! U-S-A!

Except what's good for American business isn't necessarily good for Americans. We're not just working smarter, but harder. And harder. And harder, to the point where the driver is no longer American industriousness, but something much more predatory. Productivity has surged, but income and wages have stagnated for most Americans. If the median household income had kept pace with the economy since 1970, it would now be nearly $92,000, not $50,000.

Sound familiar: Mind racing at 4 a.m.? Guiltily realizing you've been only half-listening to your child for the past hour? Checking work email at a stoplight, at the dinner table, in bed? Dreading once-pleasant diversions, like dinner with friends, as just one more thing on your to-do list?

Guess what: It's not you. These might seem like personal problems—and certainly, the pharmaceutical industry is happy to perpetuate that notion—but they're really economic problems. Just counting work that's on the books (never mind those 11 p.m. emails), Americans now put in an average of 122 more hours per year than Brits, and 378 hours (nearly 10 weeks!) more than Germans. The differential isn't solely accounted for by longer hours, of course— worldwide, almost everyone except us has, at least on paper, a right to weekends off, paid vacation time (PDF), and paid maternity leave.

To understand how we got here, let's first consider the Ben Franklin-Horatio Alger-Henry Ford ur-myth: To balk at working hard—really, really hard—brands you as profoundly un-American. Who besides the archetypical Japanese salaryman derives so much of his self-image from self-sacrifice on the job? Slacker is one of the most biting insults available in polite company.

"I am exhausted," said a "part time" college instructor in Illinois. "I can't help my son with his homework because I am grading papers until late into the night. I get up very early during the week, skip lunch to save not money but time, and the workload never lets up. My employer uses and abuses full-time employees even more so than those of us who are hourly. My supervisor, for
example, runs a large department. He was just promoted to a new, even more demanding position, but his position running the department will not be filled. He will now be doing what is a 60-to-70-hour job 'on the side.' I can't complain about overwork, because everyone is competing to get enough classes to pay the bills. If you lose a class, you lose a chunk of your paycheck. If we can't handle it, the class can always be given to another teacher who will be desperate for the work or the money."

Sure, but these are tough times—employers struggling to survive the recession are just tightening their belts, right? That's true for some. But in the big picture, the data show a more insidious pattern. Consider the charts above: After a sharp dip in 2008 and 2009, US economic output recovered nicely to near pre-recession levels—we did better than most of our fellow G-7 economies. But not so for American workers: Far more people here lost their jobs, and fewer were hired back—once the recovery began—than anywhere else.

Now, some jobs always get "rationalized" away, thanks to technological or organizational improvements—an area where, it's not jingoistic to say, the US has led its European counterparts. But that "productivity gap" has narrowed considerably, and in any case, there certainly was no dramatic tech or efficiency breakthrough between 2008 and 2010 (quite—Twitter/Facebook/FarmVille—the opposite).

What about offshoring? That's certainly a factor. But increasingly, US workers are also falling prey to what we'll call offloading: cutting jobs and dumping the work onto the remaining staff. Consider a recent Wall Street Journal story about "superjobs," a nifty euphemism for employees doing more than one job's worth of work—more than half of all workers surveyed said their jobs had expanded, usually without a raise or bonus.

In all the chatter about our "jobless recovery," how often does someone explain the simple feat by which this is actually accomplished? US productivity increased twice as fast in 2009 as it had in 2008, and twice as fast again in 2010: workforce down, output up, and here were are! No wonder corporate profits are up 22 percent since 2007, according to a new report by the Economic Policy Institute. To repeat: Up. Twenty-two (22%) Percent.

This is nothing short of a sea change. As University of California-Berkeley economist Brad DeLong notes, until not long ago, "businesses would hold on to workers in downturns even when there wasn't enough for them to do—would put them to work painting the factory—because businesses did not want to see their skilled, experienced workers drift away and then have to go through the expense and loss of training new ones. That era is over. These days firms take advantage of downturns in demand to rationalize operations and increase labor productivity, pleading business necessity to their workers."

How does corporate America have the gall? You pretty much know the answer, but for official confirmation let's turn to Erica Groshen, a vice president at the Federal Reserve Bank of New York: It's easier here than in, say, the UK or Germany "for employers to avoid adding permanent jobs," she told the AP recently. "They're less constrained by traditional human-resources practices [translation: decency] or union contracts." In plainer English, here's Rutgers political scientist Carl Van Horn: "Everything is tilted in favor of the employers...The employee has no leverage. If your boss says, 'I want you to come in the next two Saturdays,' what are you going to say—no?"

And lest CNBC hornswoggle you, this is not just a product of the recession. Throughout the past decade, salaries stagnated and workloads grew, but Wall Street's bubble allowed us to drown our sorrows in credit. Then came the crash, and the speedup...speeded up.

Low-Income Workers and Families

Working Families Pay Too Much in State and Local Taxes . Remember when a presidential nominee famously said, "Forty-seven percent of Americans pay no income tax" .... ? According to the Tax Policy Center, that was the approximate fraction of households that paid no federal income tax for 2009. But, as the Tax Policy Center went on to explain, almost two thirds of the 47 percent work and contribute payroll taxes that help finance Social Security and Medicare. The temporarily unemployed, those who used to work and have now retired, those who make too little to be subject to the income tax, and entrepreneurs whose businesses experience a loss may not be paying income tax or payroll tax in a particular year but will have contributed a great deal in over time. And let's not forget the wealthy and big corporations who exploit loopholes to avoid taxes.

The House of Representatives passed H.R. 30, a bill to chip away at the Affordable Care Act's requirement that employers provide health coverage for employees who work at least 30 hours a week, amending it so that employers would only be required to provide health insurance coverage to those who work 40 hours per week.

Genius organizer Ai-Jen Poo often talks about how home care workers and other domestic workers are the invisible workforce – performing life-sustaining work for low wages and no benefits day in and day out. But last time in St. Louis at the Home Care Workers Rising conference home care workers made their dreams and their struggles highly visible. They came together from across the country to hammer out plans for a better future for themselves, their children, and the consumers for whom they provide care.

A majority of the Senate voted to proceed to debate on the Paycheck Fairness Act, a bill that would strengthen current laws against wage discrimination and make it easier for women to ensure that their employers are paying them fairly. A vote on the merits of this bill is long overdue, and Senate passage would be a critically important step forward.

But the Paycheck Fairness Act is not the only bill that could help close the gap between women's and men's earnings — which hasn't budged in a decade, as women working full time, year round are still typically paid just 77 cents for every dollar paid to their male counterparts. One reason for this persistent wage gap is that women are overrepresented in low-wage jobs: for starters, they make up two-thirds of minimum wage workers. Another bill, the Fair Minimum Wage Act, would boost pay for these workers by gradually raising the federal minimum wage from $7.25 to $10.10 per hour, increasing the tipped minimum cash wage from $2.13 per hour to 70 percent of the minimum wage, and indexing these wages to keep up with inflation.

Obama mentioned it a half-dozen times in his State of the Union address, and House Speaker John Boehner recently told Obama to "stand up for middle-class jobs." Pundits cheer the middle class. Politicians praise its virtues. Google says it has been called the "backbone of the country" at least 2.3 million times. From gridlocked Washington to cities and towns everywhere, the middle class is far and away America's favorite socioeconomic group.

Economists and sociologists say that's a big deal. Decisions are made, laws are written and elections are won or lost based on people's beliefs about the middle class and what it means to the country. A nation that so values the middle class, they say, really should be better at defining it. "It's a strange thing," said Jim Brock, a Miami University economist. "There's a large difference between what our perception of a middle-class lifestyle is and what the statistics tell us the middle is.. Strictly speaking, the median, or middle, household income in the United States today is $50,054. That's easy. The hard part is figuring out how far above or below the middle someone's income can go and still be considered middle class. Even families making six figures are "much more comfortable calling themselves 'upper middle class.' They might have a lot of money, but they don't want to feel different."

Plenty of smart people have taken a stab at that question. In the past few years, the "middle class" income range has been described as between $32,900 and $64,000 a year (a Pew Charitable Trusts study), between $50,800 and $122,000 (a U.S. Department of Commerce study), and between $20,600 and $102,000 (the U.S. Census Bureau's middle 60% of incomes).

Psychologist Ken Eisold, a contributor to Psychology Today, said, though, that the way people describe their social status has more to do with what's going on in their heads than in their wallets. "It's really more about identity," he said. Even families making six figures are "much more comfortable calling themselves 'upper middle class.' They might have a lot of money, but they don't want to feel different."

When Pew pollsters gave people a choice between lower, middle or upper class, 17% described themselves as upper class and 32% as lower class. When Gallup gave people more options, such as "working class" and "upper middle class," only 2% said they were upper class and 10% chose lower.

A 2008 Pew poll found that 40% of Americans with incomes below $20,000 – roughly equivalent to the poverty line – described themselves as middle class. And about one-third with incomes above $150,000 said they're middle class, too. Given a choice, people tend to lean to the middle. Donna Palmatary and Katherine Stillwell are examples. Palmatary, 49, lives with her husband in suburban Cincinnati. He's an engineer and she works part time from home. With a daughter in college, she said, it takes $75,000 to $125,000 for a family to live comfortably. Stillwell, 60, lives alone in Dayton, Ky., and relies on help from her grown children to get by. She is disabled after years of work as a truck driver and lives on a fraction of the income she once did. Both women say they're part of the middle class. "I always considered myself middle class, not just because of finances but because of the way we lived," Stillwell said. "I still do. It's mostly attitude."

Lifestyle also matters to Palmatary. She said frugality, a focus on family and a desire to see your children do better than you all are middle-class traits. Income matters, too, she said. Middle-class families must earn enough to maintain a house, own a car and provide a comfortable life for children. "You have to work for what you have," Palmatary said. "I don't think anybody in the middle class would call themselves wealthy. That's Donald Trump or Martha Stewart or Warren Buffett." So if Trump is at the top of the heap, where is the middle?

Economists often start with the middle 20% of the country – people earning between $39,000 and $63,000 a year – and work their way out. Some then stretch the definition to include the middle 60%, which has an income range of $20,600 to $102,000. Because that's a wide range, other factors come into play: home ownership, savings, a college education. None of those calculations, however, generates a concrete description of what is – or is not – a middle-class household.

Globalization and technological advances began to reverse the growth of the middle class. The manufacturing base in the United States changed, as good-paying jobs in factories and heavy industries went overseas to lower-paying markets and labor unions lost much of their ability to bargain for high wages and good benefits. Later, white-collar jobs from accounting and data entry to reading medical images and answering telephones in call centers were also sent offshore. Many jobs that remained in the U.S. were eliminated by computers and other technological advancements that increased productivity.

To achieve or maintain a middle-class lifestyle, many households became two-income families. Achieving middle class goals became more difficult as employers eliminated their pension plans and defined-benefit plans, the cost of a college education continued to rise and the cost of healthcare jumped. For most of the 20-year period following 1990, the Commerce Department reports that real median income grew at a rate of about 20%, while the cost of a college education grew between 43% and 60%, the cost of housing rose 56% and healthcare costs jumped by 155%.

Although there are significant challenges to obtaining middle class status, there are some proactive steps that can help make the dream a reality. Budgeting is one of the most obvious. Understanding where your money goes each month can help you determine the exact makeup of the benchmarks you are trying to match.

Planning is another crucial step. Are the kids going to a state university or a private college? Are scholarships an option? Some savvy families find money for college by participating in programs which can aide families with the costs related to sending a child to university.

Working is another one of the requirements. A second job or a side business might be just what you need to boost your income and achieve some of your goals. Putting your money to work is also an important consideration. Investing has helped build wealth for generations. In fact, income earners ranked in the top 1% enjoyed significant increases in wealth even as the middle class fell into decline. Most of that wealth came from investments. Even if you don't have the means to invest for current income, you can take a few dollars from each paycheck and save for your retirement.

Don't underestimate the role of hard work and luck. Sometimes being in the right place at the right time or taking one particular course of action over another can make all the difference. So keep watching for opportunities and make the most of them when you find them. As motion-picture mogul Samuel Goldwyn said, "The harder I work, the luckier I get." If in every society we find that work plays an important role in sustaining people's life, rule and regulation are crucial for the proper functioning of our society. The next chapter will be about rule and regulation that governs our community.

Chapter 6

Play by The Rules

It always goes unnoticeable that the law is an integral part of our life. Many people fail to understand that the same way they need so many different important things to live their lives, laws and regulations need to be at the center of human scope to regulate our action. Law is nothing new to the human race. We find the first law at the creation when God first created Adam and placed him in the garden He said, "Then the LORD God took the man and put him into the garden of Eden to cultivate it and keep it. The LORD God commanded the man, saying, 'From any tree of the garden you may eat freely; but from the tree of the knowledge of good and evil you shall not eat, for in the day that you eat from it you will surely die'." When we look at the definition of "law" it is nothing but rules that are enforced to govern behaviors.

God was good in his creation as the creator of the universe, He knows that human beings cannot function without being under the law, that's why He makes sure that every single individual experiences an equal share of the law, imprinted upon the heart of every human being is something written there by the very finger of God. "Indeed, when Gentiles, who do not have the law, do by nature things required by the law, they are a law for themselves, even though they do not have the law." (Roman 2:14) We call that "the law of conscience." That biblical verse is pretty much telling us that the law of God is written upon our consciences. In our spirit, we know right from wrong. Our mind continually argues with our spirit. The mind tells us it is acceptable to do wrong. Our conscience fires back that we are still wrong.

It is our nature to fight our conscience, trying to justify our sin and wrong. We enjoy sin because each of us is born with a sinful nature. Yet this law of God written in our conscience is a special friend. Typically we argue with our conscience so long that we no longer are able to hear what it is saying to us, although it continues to speak. If we are in compliance with the law of our conscience, there is no doubt government law and other institutional rules will be a problem in our lives.

Immigrating into a new country involves a whole learning process that includes learning the law and regulations. Not only laws are different from country to country, from region to region, but even in the very same country laws change from time to time. If we have that many people who are native born and find it difficult to keep up with all the laws, how much harder will you find it to learn or familiarize yourself with them as a new immigrant? But it's something that we must do because when we don't know the law, we will eventually violate it and pay the price for that. The price may be big or small depending of the nature of the violation. We need to get right with the law.

One thing you don't want to see happen to you as an immigrant is to go to jail and have a record. Of course, the United Stated is a country of immigrants, but immigrants who want to play by the rules and abide by the laws. Having a clean record is significantly important in the process of establishing yourself in the country. Your record can be looked at as your passport may be in some transition while you are during your livelihood in America. Consequently, if you fail to keep your record clean, not only may you lose your civil rights but you may also not be able to find the least important job in this country. People often forget about their value; we should never forget what we stand for as immigrants. Immigrants contribute greatly to the U.S economy. Statistics reveal that most of the U.S manufacturing companies belong to immigrants or children of immigrants. If we forget who we are and let our emotions or our actions put us in conflict with the law, the result can be very catastrophic to us and to our generations to come. We must avoid doing certain things which suspiciously can be a violation of the law. In addition, we need to stay alert to any changes of the law, by doing so, it helps us stay in conformity with the law. Here are some tips about how to stay in compliance with the law:

Follow your instincts.

You may have gotten into trouble in the past because you didn't follow your instincts. If your instincts are telling you that something is a bad idea, or that a person is not worth hanging out with, then you should trust your instincts and stay away. Don't be afraid to trust your gut if it's telling you to run 100 miles (160 km) in the other direction. If you have a sense that something is wrong, even if you can't pinpoint why, then chances are, you're right. In general, if a friend suggests that you do something and you have to question it even once, then it's time to back off.

Spend time with your family

As long as your family is a place where you feel safe and loved, you should spend as much time as you can with the members of your family so that you are surrounded by positive influences. Sure, it may not feel cool to have movie night with mom and dad or to help your kid sister with her science project, but your family will always be there for you, and it's important to build a healthy bond with your family members as much as you can. When you're hanging out with your family, you won't have a chance to get in trouble, will you? It's really true that idle hands make the devil's work, and the more time you spend with your family, the less time you'll be spending looking for and getting into trouble. Make a weekly routine for yourself. Have family nights every weekend, time for doing chores during the week, and time for helping out your siblings at least once or twice a week.

Avoid the wrong people

The people who may be getting you in trouble may be your very best friends. If that's the case, then it's time to find some new best friends. Sure, that may not be what you wanted to hear, but if you really want to stay out of trouble, then you can't hang out with the same people who got you into detention. Sure, if you and all of your friends have decided to stay out of trouble together, that's another thing, but how often does that happen? It's time to slowly back away from the people who are causing you to harm your own reputation as kindly and as politely as possible. You may think that you can decide to stay on track while staying friends with people who are always getting into trouble, but unfortunately, you'll still be associated with them, and will be much more likely to get in trouble for something they did, even if you were innocent. Nobody said this was fair.

Make friends who are positive influences

If you're friends with people who are good students, have meaningful goals, and live positive lives, then you're very likely to have them rub off on you. If you're only friends with negative troublemakers, then you're much more likely to be one. Though it may be hard to immediately find new friends who are doing great in school, look around your classes or your neighborhood and see if you can find people who seem nice, friendly, and willing to take in a straggler. Soon, you'll see that you're staying out of trouble by doing fun things with new, like-minded people. You can find these friends in clubs or sports teams (more on that in the next section) or by participating in a variety of other activities.

Develop positive relationships with your teachers.

Another great way to stay out of trouble is to develop a strong bond with your teachers, or at least some of them. This doesn't mean you have to suck-up to them or try to be their best friend, but it does mean that you should be a good student, show up to class on time, come in for extra help, and ask useful questions during class to show that you care. If you're off to a rough start with some of your teachers, know that you can win them over with enough hard work and effort, even if it does take time. Being on your teacher's good side is an excellent way to stay out of trouble. If they like you, they will be less likely to punish you or to find fault with you.

Find a role model

Having a role model that you really look up to can help you succeed and to make the right decisions. Your role model can be your mom or dad, an older sibling, a teacher at school, a family friend in the neighborhood, a club, or a church leader, a grandparent, or really anyone who inspires you to do well in life. You can come to this person for advice on how to not only stay out of trouble, but on how to do something meaningful with your life. A role model that you can come to regularly can end up being one of the biggest and most long-lasting influences on your life. It's important to find a person who is living a life that you admire. This doesn't mean that your role model has to be perfect -- if he or she made mistakes along the way and learned from them, then even better.

Staying Busy and Active

You may join a sports team. Joining a sports team, whether it's a team at your school or in your community, is a great way to stay out of trouble. Whether you're playing soccer, basketball, or baseball, team sports are a great way to meet interesting, athletic, and driven people and to find something to do other than get into trouble. You don't have to be the next LeBron to join a sports team and start making some meaningful connections with people. You can even focus on becoming a leader on the team so you can use even more of your energy that way. Joining a sports team will also provide you with weekly exercise, which can help you calm down and will keep you from using your energy the wrong way.

Join a club

If sports aren't your thing, you can always join a club, whether it's through regular school, your church, or another community organization. You can join an art club, chess club, French club, cooking club, debating club, or really all sorts of clubs that can help you focus on something you care about that doesn't have to do with annoying your teachers or not doing your homework. You can join a few clubs at first to get a feel of what would appeal to you the most.

Go volunteering

Volunteering is another great way to stay out of trouble and to put things in perspective. You may not be as tempted to cause a ruckus in school or in your neighborhood after you spend some time with people who are truly in need. If you're too young to do it on your own, go with a parent to a volunteering event, whether you're helping people learn to read, cleaning up a local park, or working in a soup kitchen. Find something that is meaningful to you and commit to it at least once a week. Though your schedule doesn't have to be absolutely jam packed for you to stay out of trouble, doing a few things that matter to you each week can help you focus on what is important.

Be an active student

You don't have to get straight A's to stay out of trouble -- but it certainly won't hurt you. Being an active student means showing up on time, not skipping class, raising your hand when you have questions, and doing the work in advance so you can participate. If you focus on being a good student, then you can stop thinking about ways to annoy your teachers or your parents. Find a few subjects that you really care about and work on knowing as much as you can about them. You don't have to find absolutely everything interesting, but picking at least one or two subjects that mean something to you can make a difference. Set goals for improving your grades. You don't have to get perfect scores on every test, but you can aim to go from a B to a B+ average in Math, for example.

Read as much as you can

Reading can help you improve your vocabulary and comprehension skills, become more knowledgeable and intelligent, and to see the world in a whole new way. What's more, if you're reading, then you're not getting into trouble. Getting truly immersed in a story or stories can help you forget the hours passing by and to be transported to a whole new world -- a world where you're just an observer. Start by reading for just 20 minutes before bedtime every night can help you develop an addictive lifelong habit. Read a variety of books, from science fiction to fantasy, to see what genres you like the most.

Create something

Getting creative is another great way to stay out of trouble. You can write a play and perform it with your friends, write a story, draw something, make a ceramic pot, decorate your room as if it were a rainforest, and accomplish a number of other creative tasks. Using your mind to create something completely new and original is a great use of your energy and will keep you from getting creative when it comes to following the rules. You can even sign up for an art class after school, or ask your art teacher if she has any extra projects in store for you.

Don't gossip

One way to avoid any kind of conflict is to not gossip, whether you're gossiping about your teachers, your classmates, your friends in the neighborhood, or even your cousins. Gossiping about other people only sends bad vibes, and this will inevitably get back to people in the end. You should focus on saying positive things about people, even if nobody else is feeling very positive, if you want to stay out of trouble. If you're saying bad stuff about people, it's more likely that it will eventually get back to them. And if it does, you may be in for some big trouble.

Don't try to reason with unreasonable people

One of the reasons you may be getting into trouble is because you find the need to defend or explain yourself to people who just aren't willing to listen. If you and a kid in your gym class or down the street just don't get along, then stay away. Resist the urge to set the record straight, tell people why they're acting poorly, or just to stick your head somewhere where it doesn't belong. Instead, get as much distance between you and "volatile" or annoying people as possible, and you'll be much more likely to stay out of trouble. Reasoning with people who don't want to hear it is guaranteed to get you nowhere, fast. It's a waste of both time and energy.

Avoid fighting

Obviously, if you're the kind of person who always gets into fights, then this is easier said than done. But if you really want to stay out of trouble, then you have to know how to walk away from a fight. If someone is trying to provoke you, calling you names, or just getting all up in your face, learn to take deep breaths, walk away, and keep your cool. Pouncing on those people, getting hurt, and getting sent to the principal's office or to your room is just no fun, so the next time the opportunity to fight presents itself, remind yourself that, even if it may feel good to punch someone for a few seconds—long term, it will only do you harm. Literally, just walk away. If someone is coming at you, put your hands up and leave. This does not make you a coward -- it makes you smart.

Be polite to everyone

Being kind and polite can go a long way in helping you stay out of trouble. Say "please" and "thank you" and be polite to everyone, from a random neighbor who passes by you every morning to the crossing guard. Developing a habit of good manners and good social skills will help you throughout your life, and it's a great way to keep yourself out of trouble. If you're rude or mean to people, you'll develop a reputation for being a bad seed, and no one will be in your court when you are called into question. This means be nice to your family members, too. Don't think that they know you too well for you to really be polite around them.

Take good care of yourself

You may not think that getting enough rest, eating three healthy meals, and getting some form of exercise every day has anything to with staying out of trouble, but you're wrong. Taking care of your body means you're taking care of your mind, and if your body and mind are in good shape, you're less likely to act out or get in trouble; for example, if you're hungry or exhausted from staying up all night playing video games, you're much more likely to say something rude to an adult without meaning to.

To be on the other side of the road, you may be punished for your action. Although it seems that people like to punish, there's a critical limitation to this research. Punishment is typically the only option made available for righting a wrong. It is either punish, or accept the transgression. It's possible, however, that people prefer to restore justice without punishment, focusing instead on the needs of the victim. Because researchers typically don't offer non-punitive options, we didn't know—until now—how punishment stacked up against other ways of righting wrongs. A recent set of studies from our lab has found people may strongly prefer non-punitive options when restoring justice.

A study revealed, instead of punishing, participants overwhelmingly preferred to compensate the victim through monetary means in a case after being hurt by someone. While that's not particularly surprising, participants also felt that this was enough to right the wrong: they generally didn't punish the transgressor—even when punishment was free and easy to do. This is straightforward evidence that sometimes, for some crimes, victims do not want to punish the perpetrator if there are other paths to justice. There is evidence for this in the real world as well: programs that prioritize victims' needs and foster dialogue between victims and perpetrators show the highest rates of victim satisfaction and offender accountability.

Victims, however, typically don't decide the fate of their perpetrators: judges and juries do. A core tenet of our own legal system is that victims are partial and thus should not be deciding the fate of their perpetrators. In contrast, third parties like judges and juries, are considered to be impartial and can more objectively and dispassionately mete out justice. Given these assumed asymmetries between how victims and third parties approach justice, we examined whether an individual's perspective matters when deciding how to restore justice. Would third parties (juries) sanction social transgressions differently than those who had been personally affected (victims)?

To address this, participants in a series of follow-up studies were asked to make decisions on behalf of other people. Effectively, we asked participants to act like juries—doling out punishment to the perpetrator or compensation to the victim despite having no .skin in the game. Unlike victims, third parties chose the most retributive option in our task, where the victim is compensated and the transgressor is simultaneously punished. To simplify it, although participants rarely punished transgressors after being treated unfairly, when they saw someone else being wronged, they chose the harshest form of punishment, implementing the classic "eye for an eye" form of retributive justice.

This finding sheds a new light on how people choose to rebalance the scales of justice. When we ourselves have been slighted, we appear to tend to our own needs rather than pursue punishment, but this changes when we make decisions on behalf of someone else: for bystanders or jurors, an eye-for-an-eye may be preferable. Our notion of justice seems to depend on where we stand. This leaves us with a challenge: there may be a gap between what we as victims want, and what third parties decide for us, calling into question our blind reliance on the putative impartiality of juries and judges.

American justice has not always been that way. "Life isn't fair" is a favorite saying among conservatives. And the often unspoken corollary is, "So get used to it." But most people do not want to get used to it. In fact, the desire for fairness is as American as apple pie—it is in our blood. We get riled up when people are not treated fairly and we think something should be done about it. And more often than not, the place that people turn to try to right these wrongs—to make life fairer for themselves and others—is government. Government is the main provider of justice and fairness in American society. Many government policies and government institutions are explicitly designed to promote these important public values.

The most obvious manifestation of this is the criminal and civil justice system. It is the primary way we as a society ensure that criminals are punished and that wrongs are righted. This kind of legal justice is not something that can be reliably provided by the private sector. We would not want, for instance, for there to be a market in legal justice. We would not want this justice to be something provided to the highest bidder. In fact, those times when our current justice system does take on the characteristics of a market – such as when the rich are able to get off because they can afford to hire the most talented and expensive lawyers—are exactly the times when we think the justice system has broken down. Justice should not be for sale, it must be available to all people equally, and only government can provide that.

Nor can we rely on people acting outside of the law, either individually or in private groups, to provide justice in our society. All too often the result of this kind of approach is the revenge killing, the lynch mob, or the drive-by gang shooting. Justice administered outside of government and outside of the law is almost always arbitrary, inappropriate, violent, and out of control. For justice to be true justice it must be ordered by law and administered by the government.

It is revealing that even libertarians and other anti-government ideologues admit that the criminal and civil justice systems are parts of government that are absolutely necessary and cannot be done away with. They argue that running the police, the courts, and prisons are legitimate public endeavors that must be maintained even in a minimal version of government. But there is hardly anything "minimal" about the extent and costs of this justice system. It is hardly "small" government at all. The caseloads in our courts are enormous. Over 338,000 civil and criminal case filings were made in federal district courts in 2008. State courts handled nearly 28 times as many civil cases and 82 times as many criminal cases as did the federal system—with their case filings totaling over 12 million. Of course the vast majority of these cases were settled and did not come to trial, but these numbers give us a good idea of the enormous workload being put on our court system.

The legal justice system is also hardly "minimal" if we look at how many people it employs and how much money it cost the taxpayers. In 2006, 2.4 million people were employed in the justice systems administered at the federal, state, county, and city level. These include the police, prosecutors, judges and other staff in the judicial system, and those working in corrections facilities. And in 2006, the nation spent a total of $214 billion on criminal and civil justice services. In short, government endeavors to establish and maintain a criminal and civil justice system are neither simple nor cheap, they are massive and very expensive. They require a healthy and adequately funded government.

Do you believe in justice? That our civil liberties should be protected? That all citizens should all be treated as equals? You would probably answer, "Of course!" But do you also realize that if you are an avid supporter of public values like "justice, liberty and equality," then you should also be an avid supporter of government? Government is often the only institution that can make these kinds of core political values a reality. In fact, without an active and healthy public sector, these kinds of public values would be in very short supply. Take justice, for instance. It is not usually something provided by the marketplace or created by the actions of individuals. More often it is something that can only be provided and sustained in the public sphere by the actions of government organizations like the courts and the legislatures. If we want a just society, we must work through government to get it.

This argument—that government is an essential mechanism for realizing vital public values—is an important one in making the case for government. Government is good, not simply because it provides us as individuals with certain services and benefits, but also because it is the main way to promote important values that are good for us as a whole—values that are in the public interest. This view of government as the insurer of core democratic values is one that goes back to the very beginning of our national political institutions. Consider, for example, the political sentiments expressed by the founding fathers in the preamble to the U.S. Constitution:

We the People of the United States, in Order to form a more perfect Union, establish Justice, insure domestic Tranquility, provide for the common defense, promote the general Welfare, and secure the Blessings of Liberty to ourselves and our Posterity, do ordain and establish this Constitution for the United States of America.

From the outset, the American government was primarily seen as an indispensable means of establishing and promoting certain universally recognized public values, such as justice, tranquility, and liberty. And today, as citizens, we need to recognize in government what the founding fathers saw in it: that it is the only institution we can rely on to nourish and protect these kinds of values in our society.

Governments also try to actually reduce risk rather than just spread it around, and this usually involves some kind of regulatory policy. Environmental policies lower the risk that we will be poisoned by the air we breathe or the water we drink. Consumer regulations protect us from unscrupulous businesses that would cheat us or sell us dangerous products. Other rules minimize the workplace dangers and diseases. Governments also engage in regulating the larger economic system itself. This core value being recognized worldwide, people from all over the world coming to America to enjoy life, find better opportunity and invest their monies in our businesses. According to statistics, most American businesses are owned by immigrants and this is what the next chapter is about.

Chapter 7

Be a Business-Minded Person

As we come to the last chapter of this book—one of the most important chapters that will lead you to your final destination. It's important to place an emphasis on business-minded people. To find out how to get rich, be a millionaire and create wealth that lasts. Now you can finally end your money worries for good. And the best news is anyone can learn how to become rich for life, create wealth that lasts and learn how to become a millionaire. All you need is self-belief, then just follow and practice the simple techniques to wealth creation. Best of all news is that it's easier than you think and very nice and very rewarding financially and emotionally when done. The vast majority of people are destined to be stuck in a poverty trap of long life, Wow! Is it not shocking !! The vast majority of people are destined to live unfulfilled, poor lives. Yet deep down inside their dream of getting rich is becoming a Millionaire and the creation of sustainable wealth. It is a widely documented fact that most people not only never become rich, but even worse, actually face money problems their whole lives!

Most people never build enough wealth or create enough income to adequately provide for themselves and their families. To make matters worse, even fewer people (3%) can provide for a comfortable life (not to mention rich!) in retirement. Personally, I think it is shocking and deeply regrettable! Having lived a life of daily toil, to struggle to get by with little or nothing to show for all this effort in the end. Does this sound like you?

If you are like me .... nobody taught you about money or financing when you were younger. Most of what you have learned in school or college is quite useless when it comes to making money and becoming rich. Most people will never build enough wealth and create enough income to support themselves and their dependents well during their life. Many spend most of their adult life working 60/80 hours a week, struggling to pay the bills and their mortgage, and struggle to provide for their children. Here are some disturbing facts:

90% of people will be broke within 3 months of losing their jobs. Only 3% of people take their financially independent retirement at 65. 98% of people who are poor never receive good financial advice or training throughout their lives

With our way to get rich for life, our book is not only helping you create wealth, but you can immediately know how to end the life of poverty fear and money worries you may have been experiencing. We believe that wealth creation is at the heart of the very purpose of life. The real purpose of life is to create it yourself, you can do it and everyone can do it. I can assure you that there are a lot of opportunities that you can immediately take advantage of. I highly recommend that.

Most people who are highly educated but have useless information. Having a traditional education does not make you rich. In fact, most of the richest people in the world have never gone to college and many have never even finished high school. They all have one thing in common such as an insatiable desire, the spirit and especially the tools and techniques to generate enormous wealth. Deciding to take possession of your personal development and financial education, learning the mechanisms of money and wealth creation is a vital step on your journey to wealth creation.

it's important for you to know some strategies like technical debt elimination reduction / debt, how to reduce and eliminate debt. Real Estate / Investment ... why and when is the property the ideal investment. From, growth and development of a business ... how to become a true leader in business. Retirement planning ... know how much you need to retire and how to plan. Savings and investment strategies ... how to save and invest to create wealth quickly. Making money on the Internet ... discover an online business person and marketing techniques. Investment Strategies Stock Exchange ... how to invest so that you save your assets and maximize your returns. Success Secrets ... know what it takes to succeed in just about everything.

To understand how to become rich, we must not reduce the concept of money investment. You must invest in yourself—you cultivate, train, and allow time for the implementation of your ideas. Investing your capital is also a precondition for learning how to become rich. Investing your capital is about taking risks, taking the risk to follow your reasoning, your intuition, your idea. Take the risk of losing all or part of your capital to earn a little more financial independence

There are many people out there giving advice that is based on theory, but that never happened in the real world. What you get from this book is an invaluable insight which will help put more money in your bank account and create wealth that lasts. It's unfortunate, but ... You cannot count on your job, you cannot count on your government, you cannot rely on your financial advisors to
make you rich; they can only rely on themselves. That is why it is so important that you begin today to acquire the knowledge, skills and tools to ensure your financial future. A qualified source of confidence and experience to provide guidance on the right way to get rich and develop lasting wealth. An easy to follow book that gets you started on your journey to become rich is spirit and belief in knowing that you really and finally found a source for you to get rich for life and create wealth that lasts.

That's why we've gathered insightful information based on our own experience and the experiences of countless successful people to generate real wealth and wealth secrets as they accessed information and put it into action. These intuitive secrets have created millionaires, multi-millionaires and even billionaires for those who believe and apply them to their lives.

Do not waste time on silver, do what the "average Joe" is !. They think and act differently than the average person does. They invest in their future rather than trying to spend their way to happiness. They learn by reading books on wealth creation, attending seminars, etc. They invest in assets that will make money for them while they sleep. They think long-term rather than short term. Once you start to implement some of the secrets, you soon find you are managing your money better and showing more profit in your business.

In this saying we often tend to see the will to power rather than the power of the will. Assimilate this sentence, interpret the essence. These three words are not used to blame you, but you put your foot in the door in your quest of how to get rich. You do not become rich by following others. It goes by making different choices. If 10 people walking at the same speed must get from point A to point C so they will all arrive at the same time. If you're the 11th person and you decide to walk faster, take another path, to use a means of transport ... then you will arrive before the others. Folks, it is almost impossible to be successful by solely working for people. It's understood that when you first start you may need to work for people to make some money to begin, but the notion of continuously working for people with the intention of becoming rich one day is still under study and research. You need to take initiative to be your own boss one day. That's the ultimate path to success—to be rich or be a millionaire. You need to be an entrepreneur.

Many people want to start their own business. Their main motivation: independence. Why not just get rich. It is also necessary to have the right recipe! Get rich by creating your own business may sound crazy, but it is possible to believe on the one hand the evolution of the number of people who became rich by creating their own company, and on the other, the "success stories " of entrepreneurs who started from scratch and who built "empires." So what are the keys to being part of the club?

A study revealed 40% of businesses do not survive the third year. This leaves much scope for success and getting rich by becoming an entrepreneur since the other hand 60% of newly created companies live beyond the third year of operation.

The main reasons for failures to become rich by creating your own business are:
• Lack of experience in the field covered
• The funding shortfall

We cannot fail to remind you of the importance of these two parameters critical to the success of a business venture. Since we must always find a scapegoat, the heads of failed business will not have difficulty in putting the blame on the administrative and management constraints that justify their bankruptcy.

How to become rich by creating your own business?

Marketing primarily includes all means of action that achieve and sell to prospective clients. Marketing is not advertising, because advertising is just one of the ways to market. Marketing is everything that helps make the product more appealing. For example: visiting cards, product brochures or presentation of the company, the outfits, the premises, etc. Of course, marketing is not everything and the content is as important as the shape, otherwise customers would quickly become disillusioned. It's also difficult to get rich by creating a business without customers. Contrary to popular belief, marketing can be employed with little means but with a lot of ideas for newly created companies; for example by using a strong name. As another example, consider two ice cream vendors. On the window of the first is listed only "ice-cream" and the second "ice cream sales" Enter the exotic flavors of ice cream to your desires." From which of the two are you going to buy your ice cream? The second ice-cream is marketing while the first does not do his job. To become rich by creating a business, is knowing your job, you must have a marketing strategy. After the successful capture of customers, you must retain them, which is called customer loyalty.

Many books have been written about it, but for simplicity we take the examples of the glacier. If the glacier results in loyalty cards that allow the Ice purchased to be offered by the tenth of the money with two movie tickets, the customer will return often to eat ice cream and actually be promoting the business. This procedure makes it possible to build customer loyalty and even strengthen it.

Even better, using leverage can generate more money with customer loyalty. Let's again take the example of the glacier. Consider this time that the glacier has included a coupon for a 15% discount. In addition to loyalty cards, the customer uses the 15% discount card at his next ice cream purchase, provided that it is used within 2 weeks after the first purchase. Ultimately the glacier increases its customers' frequency of visits. Furthermore, there is a good chance that the client does not return alone. It is simple, that even a reduced cost would develop into sales and increase its chances of getting rich quick while using simple ideas.

Can everyone be successful?

This is a question that comes up regularly because many people seem to doubt their ability to succeed and achieve their goals. We can effectively ask the question whether or not everyone can actually have the same chance for success, Whatever the starting point, the course, the social, physical or psychological, it is possible for everyone to succeed in their dreams, transforming their life, or achieving a specific goal.

Succeed, regardless of conditions

Obviously everyone will not be president. First, because everyone does not want it and because there is not enough room for everyone! However, one thing is certain, based on my long personal and professional experience: everyone can have a successful life, happiness, fulfilling and becoming rich because if success depended on external conditions alone, none of those successful people out there would have succeeded. There are millions of examples of people living in extreme or difficult conditions that could not only manage to get out, but also lead an exemplary life. Location, conditions of psychological or physical condition may for some be a terrible handicap, but they can also be a powerful engine for others. Throughout my career, I've seen lots of people radically transform their lives. They were simply given the means to change their way of seeing.

Success can be scientifically proven

Science has proven in recent decades that the brain is highly malleable, if we can juggle its capabilities. It is perfectly possible to change mental patterns, create new nerve connections which, in turn, will induce new behavior. Indeed, through adequate training based on concentration techniques, relaxation, meditation, autosuggestion and visualization it is perfectly possible to "reprogram" the brain and so redirect its life and move toward success, happiness and health.

Naturally, these techniques are not enough to make you think that your life will be changed and make you successful. This requires a regular and diligent practice that gradually gives us the ability to use and modify many mental and behavioral habits.

It is through repetition that new nerve connections will be created. Believing that change will happen in a few sessions is nonsense. If you exercise you know that it is a matter of repetition that a move becomes a reflex. It is inconceivable to learn to speak English in only one course. There is no discipline exception to this rule and success is a habit that is acquired. Similarly, according to the history and origins of each, we do not benefit from the same field, or the same starting point; i.e., before planting the seeds, we must prepare the soil, we will have work to do to make it suitable for their accomplishment. Some will just focus on their aspirations and set out for all their success., in other words, some will have to produce more effort and patience before seeing the beginnings of success. But if we keep this in mind, we can understand that if we maintain its efforts, of course by adjusting and modifying them as it is reasonable to expect, that sooner or later we will reach our goal.

As we have seen, we must create a favorable environment for the development of our desires, because this environment is our own mind. It must be in perfect agreement with what we want to see. Other than that, to succeed we must bring to this field some elements that will make it conducive to the development of our aspirations.

Among those elements, inspiration is very essential. We must indeed be inspired by our subject, what we want to accomplish. It must have meaning to us. Otherwise, it means that if we are to succeed for the wrong reasons, it is one of the main causes of failure because we are not in agreement with ourselves.

There is also another source of inspiration that we must not overlook: the others!
Indeed, we need to build on the success of others, people who embody for us a real success, regardless of the area of interest. Such persons, if they succeeded, understood what was needed to achieve this. We can learn much from them. I developed a habit that has been helped me and it continues helping me: "Take advice from those who have succeeded in the field that interests me." I am always listening to what people tell me, but if someone gives me bad advice, I will not pay attention to it.

It would be insufficient to give you everything you need to succeed and fail to mention things that can impact you along the road. It's crucial to lay down many different obstacles that prevent people from moving on and how to avoid them. Successful life obviously requires a tremendous amount of self-control (or huge luck). In this insatiable quest for success, we can all count on a combination of high movement from our brain. In fact, the human brain is a wonder that science has a long and hard time explaining, and which allows us to train reasoning prowess and efficiency. Nevertheless, our brain is still far from perfect, and those who regularly trust it without thinking know what I am talking about. Our brain makes many mistakes without even realizing it. These errors are usually called cognitive biases and absolutely affect everyone. These errors are especially significant barriers to succeed in life, that's why I decided to talk about them today. You'll never get rid of your cognitive biases, however, you can greatly reduce them if you become aware.

The followings are the most common cognitive biases that could seriously hinder you if you want to succeed. Use this information to be aware of their existence and relativize your judgments.

Trying to catch persisting errors

From illogical ways, our brain allows us sometimes to think of being persistent in our error that we will reduce its size. It's like someone who plays poker, he knows that he has less chance of winning when the cards are on the table, but persists because he has already invested a significant amount. While this principle can be used in your favor, there remains a significant risk if you are in a situation of failure. When you feel entering a spiral that the outcome is clearly negative, take the time to question your first intuition and consider the possibility of stopping before it's too late. Success in life is knowing possible failures, but not to the point of sinking completely.

To judge a person on his looks

We have been told time and time again, "Clothes do not make the man." But our spirit will not let us make the best choice, when you meet someone for the first time. You categorize him/her whether you like it or not. Besides, you cannot stop it. The more people you meet, the more your brain has the ability to compare and pre-identify. Always try to go beyond your first impressions, both when they are wrong and when they are right. Even if you still feel you ae right by prejudging a person, there is a chance that the person you think stupid is destined to become your best friend, or that the relationship may help you succeed in your life.

Do something to prove his freedom

This phenomenon is more prevalent in children, but continues to affect us in a more sneaky way as we mature to adulthood. The idea is to refuse to do something on the pretext that you imposed. No matter whether you want to do this thing or not, you don't want to show people that you are taking their freedom away from them. Use proper discretion in the way you impose on someone. I have seen great leaders take random decisions for the sole purpose of imposing their decision-making status. If you have the impression that you seek to impose an action, think deeply to make sure that it is the right thing to do.

Beginner's optimism

Beginners always feel that the task he attacks will not be too difficult. The excitement often takes over the planning and analysis. What may seem bearer achievement is made to be a lack of preparation and solidity which catches up quickly This is the difference between an experienced pilot traveling at more than 200 on a circuit and a person who tests his license while trying to do the same. Successful life is, of course, based on optimism. But always beware when your optimism tackles something completely new. Try to slow down enough to not end up in a wall at 180km / h.

Hope controls the uncontrollable

Sometimes we thought we could have an influence on random external events. To declare being sure about things that could be so challenging to others goes beyond the scope of human mind and spirit. As a father of two, I see this tendency manifested in my attempts to control my children in areas where I ought to give them choices, even though they are transitional adults closing in on independence. When children are younger, we can control much of their environment, and we make many of their choices for them. We cannot protect them from every harm, but it is reasonable for parents to intervene and make choices that will help prevent serious damage. We can control where they go to school, who they play with, and what they eat. But we have to transfer that control to them, and our attempt to retain control beyond the days they are entrusted to us can only lead to long-term dysfunction and their inability to stand on their own. Seek to control (or believe that the control) you give is the assurance of a try and fast failure. Analyze all random parameters in all your projects, and build and consider the best of the worst possible cases.

Ignore that which does not support our beliefs

I could not imagine a better example than the American electoral debate to illustrate this. Whether you are in one camp or the other, you will notice that each tends to defend his party systematically denigrating what the other says. Even in the highest intellectual circles of our country, everyone seems to forget to consider the facts on both sides and to question his judgment based on reality. Human beings tend to be interested only in what sustains his thoughts.
It can sometimes unintentionally ignore a threat to its business, life and dreams just because he believes in himself. This bias has cost many people, believe me. Even if you disagree with an idea, try always to listen to and analyze it in depth. Never take anything for granted if you do not want to see your success objectives disappear forever.

Believe that you can resist temptation

We still have a lot less control over our desires as we imagine. We always think that we can leave any of our addictions whenever we want, only our brain likes the easy way and still tries to convince us that the facility is the right solution. Some people think the best way to resist temptation is to yield to it, is not it! For those who want to succeed in life, the temptations are a real threat. Beware and always control what you think, because your mind will always sell you a good reason to succumb and put you in danger. Move away from your most important temptations. If you find yourself saying that this is not a problem because you could easily stop, then you are in danger, hurry and stop!

Make an isolated event a generality

Equally annoying it may seem, is a single event that is not enough to form an opinion. Have you ever felt a sense of injustice while your boss began to judge you negatively because of an isolated action? It turns out that we are all at the origin of injustices without even realizing it. Learn how to judge an event not on the level of emotion it generates, but the likelihood that it has to recur in the future. Military American movies always say "once is a mistake, twice a coincidence and three times sabotage." Know how to distinguish these three!

Do not take the credit for our successes

It is easy for us to take credit for our successes just to maintain our esteem, but we rarely take credit for our failures. It is always the fault of another or an unexpected event. Children think good grades in school are based on our intelligence, but it requires the teacher or the course to explain our failures. In fact, it is basically impossible to be in harmony with oneself and achieve our goal if we do not accept our responsibility for our failures. Be successful, is also to recognize our weaknesses. Just take responsibility for your failures. Do not put the blame on others, accept that you fail when you fail. This is the only way forward.

Self- fulfilling prophecies

Under a complex title hides one of the most common problems of the human spirit. Always imagine the worst for the future. A person is convinced that he has no means to successfully get the job of his dreams. He does not have the means to obtain the skills required for this position and does not seek to build a network that would otherwise help his dream be realized. Believing that you will not be successful in his life is the best way not to succeed in life.

One thing successful people don't do "give up their dream"

There is no clear and definitive path to success for anyone. The most successful people in any endeavor will tell you many stories of failure within their life journeys. Many have experienced major failures, multiple times. But they never gave up. The greatest secret to success is learning how to "Fail Up." It would even be fair to say that failure is the driver that makes truly successful people even more hungry and determined to achieve their success.

Henry Ford stands tall as a pioneer of modern business, yet this founder of the Ford Motor Company failed many times on his route to success. His first business attempt at building a motor car was shuttered after just a year and a half when stockholders lost confidence in his ability to succeed. He gathered more cash and re-started his effort, but a year later he was forced out of his own company yet again. The entire motor industry had lost faith in Henry Ford, but he was not deterred. He found another investor to start the Ford Motor Company, and the rest are history.

Walt Disney DIS +0.64% – The creator of the global Disney empire of film studios, theme parks, and consumer merchandise travelled a long and winding road to success. Amazingly, Walt

Disney was fired from an early job at the Kansas City Star Newspaper because he was "not creative enough." In 1922 he launched a Kansas-based company called Laugh-O-Gram with a mission to produce cartoons and short advertising films. One year later, in 1923, the business went broke. He didn't give up, though. He moved from Kansas to Hollywood to begin another venture, and The Walt Disney Company was born.

Richard Branson – Richard Branson is a highly successful entrepreneur. Branson's successful ventures include Virgin Atlantic, Virgin Music, and Virgin Active. At age 16, however, Branson was a high school drop out with hopes of starting a student magazine. It didn't succeed. He went on to establish a mail-order record business that did so well it led to the creation of the record shop he called Virgin. Today we know him as one of the world's greatest entrepreneurs, but on his path to success he endured many more failures, including Virgin Cola, Virgin Vodka, Virgin Clothes, Virgin Vie, and Virgin Cards. Thank heavens he never gave up!

Oprah Winfrey has just returned to the No. 1 position on the Forbes celebrity list after two years in second place and a drop in income of $88 million since last year. She is broadly acclaimed as the queen of entertainment, and has enjoyed an amazing career as a talk show host, media proprietor, actress, and producer. However, Oprah began her life in poverty, and in her earlier career she endured numerous setbacks, such as getting fired from her job as a reporter because she was "unfit for television," and fired as the co-anchor of weekday news on WJZ-TV, which resulted in her being demoted to morning TV. Clearly those organizations didn't recognize the incredible talent they were squandering.

J.K. Rowling – The iconic writer of the Harry Potter series, which has resulted in the sale of more than 400 million books, is also responsible for the most successful and lucrative book-based film series in history. However, early in her career as an author, Rowling received endless rejections from publishers. Even her famous Harry Potter manuscript was rejected outright for reasons, such as, "It is far too long for a children's book." or, "Children books never make any money." Her story is even more inspiring when you realize that she was a divorced single mother living on welfare when her career as a writer began.

Bill Gates –The famous co-founder and chairman of Microsoft dropped out of Harvard to set up a business called Traf-O-Data. The partnership between Bill Gates, Paul Allen, and Paul Gilbert was based on a good idea to read data from roadway traffic counters and create automated reports on traffic flows. But the business model was flawed and the company had few customers and resulted in losses from 1974 to 1980 before it was closed. But Bill and his partner Paul Allen put the lessons they'd learned to good use when they created Microsoft.

Milton Hershey failed in his first two attempts to set up a confectionary business. But is there any of us who doesn't know and love Hershey confections and chocolate today?

H.J. Heinz began his career with a company that produced horseradish. It went bankrupt. Thankfully, he was persistent and had some other ideas in mind. His food products left his competitors far behind trying to catch up.

Steve Jobs was fired from Apple, joining a long list of brilliant leaders who have been removed from the companies they founded. He returned several years later to turn Apple into one of the most successful technology and consumer organizations in the world.

We had many more that could be used to inspire you in your journey to success, but we choose to stop here. And I'm sure many of you could add a few more names, both famous and unknown, to the list. All of them share the same successful characteristic: They never gave up, no matter how many times they had to get back up and dust themselves off before they could fully succeed. What about you?

Another thing you need to do as you seek to open a business when you come to immigrate to America. Here's some important advice:

The first thing to do is to make an active watch on your target market via the internet. Just start skillfully using business directories for knowing your competitive environment, but also keep yourself informed of business news in your industry and country. Ask your Chamber of Commerce about market research or books published in your industry. A study purchased for a few hundred dollars can save you a lot of time in understanding the target market.
Ask about the seasonal trade fairs in the country. These events allow you to identify key market players, to observe international exhibitors on site as well as the vitality of the market according to the importance of the event. You will identify your assets and the many competitors in the market. Do not limit your search to the target country, expand your watch also linguistically to neighboring or nearby countries to have an overall vision.

What is the valued added to your product / service to market?

The link between innovation and export is very strong. If your company is innovative, it is very likely, if not certain, that you have openings for export markets. Moreover, the market does not export a product that has no added value to the product locally! For a product to monetize the significant commercial investment to you in a given country, it is necessary that its added value be higher than that of local production, because an equivalent product would be surprising if you it couldn't be competitive, especially if the product is already manufactured locally! Identify your competitors in the market and their distributors or subsidiaries. This work will allow you to know the type of products, the level of technology and the level of prices accepted in the market. Of course, you must analyze the market when you choose the country. The technology used by your product: is it late, early, or in the expectations of the market?

In the case of adapting to consumer expectations, the most obvious example is the wine. In countries where consumption is recent, the market adapts first to white wine that is drunk fresh and the taste is less pronounced; then to light red. So there is indeed a degree of maturity of the market.

Focus its strategy on the client

Your strategy is it sufficiently customer-oriented?

Think back to your maxim abroad, overseas, it's you! Questioning yourself on this subject is essential. The first thing to do is to be able to communicate in the language of the country, it is both a sign of respect but also a guarantee that you will understand negotiations and discussions with your audience. Have a plate translated into English is a first step, it is translated into the language of the target country and allows the customer to avoid having to make an effort to discover your offer. The second point is to understand and adapt to the customer's mindset, culture. While the French will tend to flex technology and technical performance of its service, the American will demonstrate its ability to earn money for the potential customer. The product remains the same, but how to approach the situation is very different.

All exporters are unanimous on one point: International is a humility and simplicity school. Working or its usual use, product color, type of packaging, taste for food products ... must be able to adapt to the expectations of the customer.

A highly technical product that cannot be repaired locally or that will save labor in low-cost countries will not be adapted to the situation. Your technical skills will not be a good selling point. Automation will sometimes be resented locally when the manual work within the company sustains a village or town.

What kind of person do you have to be to become a successful entrepreneur?

In fact, anyone can become an entrepreneur. Each individual must carefully study its business plan to be sure they have the right skills and the right resources for this particular idea. To start a small retail business for example, business skills, knowledge, and capital requirements are very different from those needed to open the first branch of a franchise. Similarly, buy a franchise of a reputed brand and proven business model requires a very different approach from that required to launch an entirely new business with a brand unknown.

How to determine if I am able to start a business?

Even if you found a great idea with the best location and if everything is funded, the biggest obstacle yet to overcome. The fact that you have never done this kind of thing before. ask any seasoned entrepreneur and he will tell you that there is so much to learn that most people simply do not know where to start. Many entrepreneurs never cross the stage of the dream. Often new entrepreneurs worry so much and forget to focus on the overview of the project.

References

From Wikipedia, the free encyclopedia
http://en.wikipedia.org/wiki/Robert_Herjavec

http://www.mainstreet.com/article/5-successful-immigrant-entrepreneurs

Laurie Kulikowski. Jun 30, 2011 3:00 PM EDT

The 13 Richest Americans Of All Time". Business Insider. July 15, 2007. Retrieved January, 2015.

American Culture: Traditions and customs of the United States. By king Ann Zimmermann, Live science contributor. January 15, 2015

An adventure in Americans culture & values. Provided by Marian, Director, international Student/Scholar Office, UNC Charlotte.

The First Great Awakening. From Wikipedia, the free encyclopedia
http://en.wikipedia.org/wiki/First_Great_Awakening

wakening- Jonathan Edwards by Tony Cauchi, May 2006

http://anthro.palomar.edu/language/language_5.htm

https://www.facebook.com/permalink.php?story_fbid=169675939902637&id=169088556584552

Galaxy language solution. October 8, 2013 · New Delhi, India ·

Importance of College Education
Why it is important to go to college by Jeff
McGuirehttp://www.collegeview.com/articles/article/importance-of-college-education

Americans: Overworked, Overstressed. May by Dean
Schabnehttp://abcnews.go.com/US/story?id=93604

The Ethics of Migration and Immigration: Key Questions for Policy Makers. A Briefing Paper

by Lynette M. Parker

The One Thing Successful People Don't Do (And 9 Famous Examples) By
Dav9d K. Williams

http://www.forbes.com/sites/davidkwilliams/2012/07/24/top-10-list-the-greatest-living-business-leaders-today/

HOW A FOREIGNER CAN

BE SUCCESSFUL IN AMERICA

Be A Millionaire

FIRST EDITION

By Paul J. Toyle

www.ingramcontent.com/pod-product-compliance
Lightning Source LLC
Chambersburg PA
CBHW070915180526
45168CB00005B/2017